How to Escape the Messiah Trap

Other books by Carmen Renee Berry
When Helping You Is Hurting Me
Loving Yourself as Your Neighbor (with Mark Lloyd Taylor)

How to Escape
the
Messiah Trap

A Workbook for
When Helping You Is Hurting Me

Carmen Renee Berry

HarperSanFrancisco
A Division of HarperCollinsPublishers

FIRST EDITION

Library of Congress Cataloging-in-Publication Data
Berry, Carmen Renee.
   How to escape the Messiah trap : a workbook for When helping you is hurting me / Carmen Renee Berry. —1st ed.
     p. cm.
   Workbook based on material in: When helping you is hurting me. c1988.
   ISBN 0–06–060807–2 (alk. paper)
     1. Self-sacrifice.   2. Spiritual exercises.   I. Berry, Carmen Renee. When helping you is hurting me.   II. Title.   III. Title: Messiah trap.
   BF637.S42B47 1991 Suppl.
   158'.2—dc20   91–55009
                                                                                                              CIP

91   92   93   94   95   ❖   MAL   10   9   8   7   6   5   4   3   2   1

To
Dr. Paul Roberts,
my therapist and mentor, whose support and instruction has helped me
experience the healing that made this book possible

Contents

Acknowledgments

I am grateful for the support and significant contributions many friends and colleagues have made to the development of this workbook.

Warmest appreciation is extended to my former editor, Jan Johnson, who wisely initiated this project. I appreciate my editor, Lonnie Hull, and her assistant, Beth Weber, for overseeing the manuscript through the various stages of development. I am grateful to Rebecca J. Laird, who diligently scrutinized each draft and offered invaluable suggestions and feedback. Caroline Pincus and Jamie Sue Brooks deserve applause for transforming the manuscript into its final format.

I extend my gratitude to Roy M. Carlisle of Mills House, who contributed creativity and originality to the structural development of the manuscript. In addition, his unfailing encouragement carried me through the difficult spots in the writing process.

I am grateful to Daniel Psaute, who reviewed the manuscript and offered unique and helpful suggestions. I want to thank Dale Ryan and Patrick Means, my colleagues at the National Association for Christian Recovery, for loving me and offering support and understanding during the times I was juggling competing projects and responsibilities.

For personal support throughout this process, I express my deepest gratitude to Catherine Smith, Robert Parsons, Joel Miller, Patricia Luehrs, Bobette Buster, Irene Flores, Gail Walker, Michael Dochterman, Bill Skinner, and Bill Rich. I am especially appreciative of the acceptance and nurturance I have received from my Bodywork Support Group: Susan Latta, Kate O'Sullivan Litteken, and Virginia Frederich. In addition, I want to thank

Martin Nunez and the other gifted massage therapists at Nice to Be Kneaded for helping me relax through an ordinarily stressful process.

How to Use This Workbook

This workbook is designed to take you on a journey of recovery. My recovery began several years ago when I started a process of healing from codependency. I originally developed the exercises contained in this workbook to aid in my own recovery process. Because I have benefited from the daily discipline of these exercises, I am convinced that this workbook contains a functional and healthy model for progressing down the path of inner healing.

In the recovery field there are numerous workbooks and approaches that emphasize diverse elements. They include processes such as keeping a journal, utilizing ritual, doing bodywork, drawing, working with the inner child, focusing on support systems and relationships, and depending on a Higher Power. Rather than limit myself to one approach, I have utilized all of these recovery techniques to enliven and deepen my own healing process. Consequently, this workbook combines many avenues to recovery.

I believe this comprehensive approach is important. We all learn in different ways. Some people are visually oriented and remember what they read, while others are more oriented toward what they hear. People who are body, or kinesthetically, oriented use their senses of touch and movement to gather information. I have included exercises that will access all these ways of learning. As you work through these sessions, you will participate in reading, writing, drawing, and visualization (visual); inner dialogue and group and individual discussion (auditory); and creation of ritual, movement, and massage exercises (kinesthetic).

Another very important element in the design of this workbook is the highlighting of the relationship between inner life and outward action. Each session moves from interacting with your interior reality to implementing new insight in changed behavior and attitudes.

If you are a more introverted personality, you may be attracted to the exercises that focus on the inner life. If you are a more extroverted personality, then just the opposite may occur. My sense is that recovery is a journey of both inner and outer growth and maturation. To maximize the benefits of this workbook I urge you to engage in both the interior- and the exterior-oriented exercises. Recovery not only includes healing our inner wounds but can and should bring fulfillment and healing to our external relationships.

Each of the sessions is divided into six components: Recovery Reading, Recovery Reflection, Recovery Ritual, Recovery Expression, Recovery Celebration, and the Recovery Checklist.

Recovery Reading: The recommended reading is intended to provide a springboard for thinking and feeling, and to direct your thoughts and feelings to the task at hand in each session.

Recovery Reflection: This section will guide you into your inner life in a way that facilitates healing. These exercises are meant to take you a step at a time into your inner reality. To assist in working through the exercises, I am including examples from my own experiences. As we work with the raw material of our own thoughts and feelings, interior healing is made possible.

Recovery Ritual: This is an important step in connecting the inner work with the outer world. When you honor your inner work by creating a concrete and symbolic ritual, the changes that are occurring in your thoughts and feelings are reinforced. The use of ritual also creates a special and safe place, a place that is geographically as well as psychologically and spiritually sacred.

Recovery Expression: This section provides a variety of opportunities to develop and strengthen supportive relationships. It is an application of the inner changes that have occurred during the Recovery Reflection.

Recovery Celebration: The recovery process is hard work and often entails facing pain and grief. A critical, but often overlooked, component of recovery is celebrating the progress you have made and learning how to enjoy life one day at a time.

Recovery Checklist: The Recovery Checklist provides an overview of all that has been accomplished during the session.

The inspiration and framework for this workbook builds on material in *When Helping You Is Hurting Me.* All of us who have been caught in the Messiah Trap can finally escape its clutches when we acknowledge that we are holding onto the Trap as tightly as it is imprisoning us. To that end I have expanded the material from chapter 7 into this working process of growth. May you experience grace along the way.

Session 1

This Is My Time

Preparing for the Journey

Those of us who have fallen into the Messiah Trap believe we are on our own. Deep in our hearts, we do not feel we can trust anyone, not even God, to help us. This is because, through a variety of childhood experiences, we were taught that it was our job to take care of others in such a way that we sacrificed our own needs. In fact, we came to believe that the world was a better place when we allowed ourselves to be hurt or deprived.

The only way to escape the Messiah Trap is to reject the lies of the Trap and to learn, perhaps for the first time, to trust someone else. *No one can escape the Messiah Trap alone.* We all need others to help us through this process of healing and growth. As you move through these exercises you will be challenged to set up a new and more solid support system.

I would be honored if you would allow me to become the first member of your new support system. Even though I may not know you personally, you and I have a lot in common.

First of all, we are courageous people. While many people remain caught in their addictions, trying to dull their inner pain, you and I are facing the truth about ourselves. The fact that you have this workbook in your hand and are reading this sentence sets you apart from many people in this world. We are on the path toward recovery and healing.

Second, you and I have tried to do what we thought was right. It can be discouraging to find out that our helping activities were actually addictive, codependent, and self-destructive. It is nevertheless important to hold onto the fact that we have tried to do our best and have wanted good things for others. We are genuinely caring people. We can draw strength from our desire to love as we seek to break the grip of the Messiah Trap.

Third, you and I have been hurt. Perhaps those who damaged us so deeply did not intend to do us harm. Others may have known they were hurting us and simply did not care about our well-being. Regardless of intent, we bear the wounds from the neglect, abuse, and deception of others. These wounds have been buried deep behind our Messiah masks of competency and self-reliance.

Throughout this workbook, I would like to share some of my courage, caring, and pain with you. In response, I hope that you use this workbook to stir up your courage, rekindle your caring, and tenderly attend to your wounds.

Recovery Reading

The recommended reading: chapter 1, pages 1–7, in *When Helping You Is Hurting Me.*

Recovery Reflection

I first realized I had fallen into the Messiah Trap when, despite my trying to do everything "right," my life came crashing in around me. I had dedicated myself to the care of others while ignoring my own feelings of loneliness and despair. During the day I comforted others, but at night I was haunted by overwhelming waves of anxiety and fear. My body showed the strain of excessive caregiving through migraine headaches, flus, and a loss of appetite that resulted in rapid weight loss. My personal life was nearly nonexistent as I had no time for spontaneous intimacy. I was too busy "taking care" of people to be intimate with them.

I had placed myself high on a pedestal as a person who was in control and "in the know." When I fell off that pedestal, it was a long and painful drop back to reality.

It is easy to fall prey to the Messiah Trap because its lies are so deceptive. They may look good at first glance. After all, being a caring and helpful person is something we value. These lies are not based on genuine love, however, but on an overly developed sense of responsibility coupled with low self-esteem. The Messiah Trap hinges on a two-sided lie: side 1, "If I don't do it, it won't get done," and side 2, "Everyone else's needs take priority over mine."

Anyone can fall into the Messiah Trap by believing that he or she is indispensable on the one hand, and yet unimportant on the other. Let me give you an example of how this trap has been set for me. When I was a therapist and community outreach worker, numerous phone calls would come in to my office with each caller asking for assistance. The voice on the line would say something like, "I'm the pastor at a local church and we've just discovered that one of the children in our day-care center has been sexually abused. The family doesn't have much money to pay for treatment and yet we want the very best for this little one. You've come highly recommended and the family has agreed to work with you. They have refused to go to the local clinic. Won't you help us?"

In the back of my mind I would say to myself, "Yes, I am the best therapist in this field, this pastor is right. This child needs me and if I don't help, this child and family could suffer so much more. If I don't do it, it won't get done." I never said these things out loud because they sounded too arrogant. Instead I said something humble like, "Certainly, I'd be glad to be of service." But deep inside I believed that I was the only one who could help in this situation and, therefore, felt obligated to take on this additional burden. I was caught by the first side of the Messiah Trap: If I don't do it, it won't get done.

Requests like this one came in all day long. I was asked to serve on interagency committees, to volunteer with the youth at a local center, to bring the decorations to a friend's house for a wedding shower, to drop by the cleaners on the way home to pick up a neighbor's laundry. . . . And to all requests I said yes because I had been convinced that if I didn't do it, it wouldn't get done. I wanted to be wanted. I needed to be needed.

The next day, however, I would wake up feeling overwhelmed by all the things I had agreed to do. There weren't enough hours in the day to accomplish all I had promised. I didn't know how to say no. If I tried, an inner nagging voice would chide me, "Carmen, how can you take time off when that little child needs you? How can you say no when everyone is counting on you? How can you be so selfish?" The second side of the Messiah Trap had me in its clutches: Everyone else's needs take priority over mine.

On days when I felt strong and superconfident, I would fall prey to the first lie, If I don't do it, it won't get done. On days when I felt overwhelmed and inadequate, I was susceptible to the second lie, Everyone else's needs take priority over mine. My self-image would flip between feeling overly competent and feeling worthless. Those of us caught in the Messiah Trap struggle with these conflicting feelings.

Exercise 1:

Acknowledging We Have Been Trapped by Messiah Lie 1 (If I don't do it, it won't get done)

Describe how you have been trapped by the first Messiah lie.

How Carmen has been trapped by the first Messiah lie:

I take on more clients than I can reasonably handle because I feel that there is no one else who can or will help them. When people like the pastor call me, I feel important and special.

How I have been trapped by the first Messiah lie:

Exercise 2: ***Acknowledging I Have Been Trapped by Messiah Lie 2 (Everyone else's needs take priority over mine)***

Describe how you have been trapped by the second Messiah lie.

How Carmen has been trapped by the second Messiah lie:

I have trouble saying no to a request for help. If I refuse the pastor's request for help, I feel guilty and selfish. How can I put my needs over those of a little girl?

How I have been trapped by the second Messiah lie:

Admitting I am an addict is extremely difficult for me. I would rather believe that I am perfect, free from defect, out there helping to save the world. It is much more comforting to pretend that my compulsive helping is actually beneficial than to honestly acknowledge my addiction. When I am in the Messiah Trap, I am just as out of control as any heroin addict, just as self-destructive as any alcoholic, and just as dangerous to others as any compulsive offender.

If you are serious about breaking free of your addiction, it is critical that a regular routine of self-care be established. We Messiahs already know how to take care of everyone else. Many of us are quite sophisticated in our helping techniques. But we must go back to the basics, back to the beginning, if we are going to learn how to attend to our own needs.

It is important to create and protect a special time for ourselves. This can be difficult for us Messiahs. I make an "appointment" with myself, just as I would with any other important person in my life. I cannot leave it to chance because I naturally leave myself out.

Most of us do not feel we have the time for such a "luxury." After all, we have lunches to make, phone calls to return, memos to write, and an endless list of people who need us. If you are not prepared to allot time for yourself, however, I believe you are not yet ready to face your addiction.

Exercise 3:   *Creating Special Time for Ourselves*

To develop your plan for recovery, get out your calendar and set aside a regular time each week. If you are a morning person, early in the day may be best. For those of us who are nocturnal, an evening time is quite acceptable. Some days will be workdays and your recovery time may be scheduled during a lunch break. On the weekends, it may be better to wait until the children are in bed. Each week, set aside a regular time. Treat this appointment with yourself as you would a meeting with someone very important. You are, in fact, the most important person you know.

If someone asks to meet with you during your scheduled recovery time, tell him or her that you already have an important appointment and find a different time to see the person. Occasionally a crisis may arise that takes precedence and you may need to reschedule your recovery appointment. However, we Messiahs are so quick to give up what is ours that I want to warn you against rescheduling unless absolutely necessary. As far as I am concerned, a crisis that takes precedence over my own time is limited to a medical emergency. Merely "inconveniencing" someone else is not reason enough to give up my allotted time. Do not simply give the time away and then forget about your own needs. Treat yourself with the same respect that you treat others and reschedule yourself.

Recovery Ritual

I honor my personal time by lighting a candle at the beginning of each session. After a few moments of silence, I ask God or my Higher Power (the term used in the Twelve-Step Group movement for God according to your understanding) to join me in my recovery work. I acknowledge my need for guidance and strength. At the end of my session, I thank God for the guidance I have received and ask for the strength to follow through on what I have learned. Blowing out the candle signifies the closing of my personal recovery time.

You have just created a special place for yourself. By developing a ritual, you will more fully honor this growth. Think of a two-part ritual, one that will open and close your session.

Carmen's recovery ritual:

At the beginning of each session, I light a candle and ask God for guidance and strength. The end of the session is honored by thanking my Higher Power for guidance and strength and by extinguishing the candle.

My recovery ritual:

Recovery Expression

No recovery journey is complete until our new insights make a difference in our day-to-day lives, out in the world where we live. In this segment of our session together, we will address how we can use our insights to create healthier, more balanced relationships with those we love.

When I first scheduled my personal recovery time, my friends, colleagues, and family members were not accustomed to my being unavailable to them. Some did not understand why I would need to "be alone." Others thought it was fine, until they wanted to see me during the time I had set aside. Then I was told that I had "taken this recovery thing too far."

Step 1:
Selecting Who to Tell About My Personal Recovery Session

When I start something new in my recovery journey, I have learned to let those in my life know what it is I am doing, what I intend to accomplish, and how it may affect our relationship. I allow them time to tell me how they feel about this change, *but I do not ask their permission.* Rather, I inform them of a change that will occur and may affect their lives.

I have found that telling my friends and family about new phases of my recovery helps all of us. First, I honor their importance in my life by letting them know what is happening in my life.

Second, I honor their feelings *before* the change affects them. When the change is felt, there is often less anger or misunderstanding. I can say, "Remember we talked about the fact that I wouldn't be available from 9 to 10 AM? I will be glad to talk to you before or after that time."

Third, I give my friends and colleagues an opportunity to be supportive of my recovery process. Quite honestly, I need all the support I can get. Most of the people in my life are eager to hear about new things I have learned. Many are themselves in recovery, and we often share our new insights and growth.

While it can be helpful to share with others, it is also important to state that we are not obligated, in any way, to tell everyone we know about our private lives. We have the right to select carefully with whom we share our recovery journey.

As I thought over who I wanted to tell about my daily recovery sessions, I selected only those people who would be most affected by the change. Since I live alone, I did not need to inform a spouse or roommate. If you live in community, your routine will naturally affect those sharing your home. It is recommended that your spouse, roommate, children, or anyone else who shares your daily routine be informed of your new plan.

It was helpful for me to let my closest friends know about my private recovery time. Although they may not see me on a daily basis, it helps them to know what I am doing and why, at times, it may take a while for me to respond to a phone call.

In addition, because I work part-time at a nonprofit agency, I chose to explain the new schedule to my supervisor. My private recovery time precluded scheduling meetings and appointments during certain hours of the morning. If you decide to schedule your recovery time into your workday, you may want to inform those who work with you. It is especially important to inform the switchboard operator so that your phone calls will be diverted until your "return."

People Carmen will tell about scheduling her recovery session:

- *My close friends*
- *My supervisor*

People I will tell about scheduling my recovery session:

Name: _____   Phone: _____

Name: _____   Phone: _____

Name: _____   Phone: _____

Name: _____   Phone: _____

Step 2:
Deciding What to Tell Others About My Recovery Session

Once you have selected those you will tell, the next step is deciding what to tell them. We have no obligation to tell others about things that are private or personal. Deciding what we will say to others is an important part of learning how to properly care for ourselves and for those we are learning to love.

It is easy for me to feel guilty about taking time for myself and, if I do not prepare myself ahead of time, I sound more as if I am giving an apology than an explanation. If I am feeling guilty I may go on with something like, "You know I've been having these headaches and have been depressed lately and so I thought I'd try out this new idea of spending time alone. I think it has something to do with my childhood. Anyway, I'm going to be setting aside some time each morning, and I'll be leaving my machine on. Of course, if it's an emergency I want you to feel like you can get through to me at any moment. What do you think about this? Is it okay with you?"

If I am in an angry, resentful mood, I can blurt out something like, "I can't take it anymore! All these demands on my time! Don't call me in the morning because that is *my* time, you got it?"

Clearly, neither of these approaches is helpful to me or to those in my life. Through a variety of difficult experiences and misunderstandings, I have learned that it is best for me to prepare and even rehearse what I am going to say. Usually the shortest, simplest, and most concrete explanations are the easiest to understand and receive. To my friends, I can say something like, "Since you are a close friend, I want to share something important with you. I've allotted time each day to my own recovery. From 9 to 10 o'clock, I will be spending time working on different exercises that will help me grow. My answering machine will be on, so if you call during that time, I will be able to call you back as soon as I'm finished. I'd really appreciate your support as I commit myself to a new discipline."

Such an explanation affirms the value I place on my relationships, states clearly what decision I've made (rather than asks permission), addresses how the change may affect them, and asks for support.

I have a unique and very flexible work situation. As a writer and part-time staff member of a nonprofit recovery organization, I negotiate my hours on a weekly basis with my supervisor. Therefore, it was comfortable to say, "I am committing myself to a regular routine and would prefer to schedule my meetings and work obligations after 10 AM." As this was acceptable, a further explanation of what I was doing with my morning hours was not necessary.

What Carmen will say about her recovery session:

Friends: Since you are a close friend, I want to share something important with you. I've allotted an hour each day to my own recovery. From 9 to 10 AM, I will be spending time with myself working on different exercises that will help me grow. My answering machine will be on so that, if you call during that time, I will be able to call you back as soon as I'm finished. I'd really appreciate your support as I commit myself to a new discipline.

Supervisor: I am committing myself to a regular routine and would prefer to schedule my meetings and work obligations after 10 AM.

What I will say about my recovery session:

Now that you are prepared, call each person listed. Don't put it off. This is a necessary part of your personal recovery journey. For some on your list, a brief explanation is all that is needed. Set up appointments for those who will need more time and explanation.

Recovery Celebration

We have already accomplished a great deal together and it is only day one! We have begun an important and life-changing journey together. You have created a safe place for yourself and a plan to protect that space. A powerful ritual has been developed that honors the progress you have made. Plus, you have shared with those in your life the most important gift you have, yourself. You have allowed others to participate in your recovery process.

I have found it energizing to end a session by concentrating on what I have learned or accomplished. Look back over the exercises and pick out the parts that are especially helpful to you. Reword these insights into affirmations.

Carmen's affirmations:

1. *I am a worthwhile person.*
2. *I have a legitimate need to spend time on myself.*
3. *God is available to help me through this process.*
4. *My friends love and support me through this process.*

My affirmations:

Sit quietly with your eyes closed. Listen to your breath. Once you are in tune with your body's rhythm, meditate on these affirmations.

Recovery Checklist:

Congratulations. You have taken an important step in creating a healthy, caring lifestyle. To remind yourself of your progress, check each item you have accomplished.

- ☐ I read chapter 1, pages 1–7, in *When Helping You Is Hurting Me*
- ☐ I acknowledged being trapped by Messiah Lie 1
- ☐ I acknowledged being trapped by Messiah Lie 2
- ☐ I created a special time for myself
- ☐ I created a recovery ritual
- ☐ I selected who to tell about my recovery session
- ☐ I decided what to say about my recovery session
- ☐ I celebrated my progress

Session 2

It's My Turn

Asking for Help

Throughout this workbook I emphasize that *no one can escape the Messiah Trap alone.* To be honest with you, I still have trouble accepting this fact. It would be so much easier for me to hide away for a couple of days and take care of all this by myself. I don't like being vulnerable to other people. I am accustomed to being the one everyone else turns to in times of trouble. It isn't easy admitting that I also have needs.

Asking for help actually means developing a stronger, more reliable support system. Two essential components of that support structure are a regular support group and a counselor. I could not have come as far in my recovery as I have without a solid support system. In fact, I feel it is dangerous to attempt recovery without adequate support. It is easy to become overwhelmed or confused by the recovery process. We all need a safe place to go.

Why is it so important to attend a regular support group? Why can't we break free from the Messiah Trap on our own or with the help of a few supportive friends?

First, if we rely solely on our friends for support, we can become overly dependent on these relationships. During the difficult times that come for all of us in recovery, it is possible for us to overtax our friends' resources, needing more from them than they can reasonably give. We need to be mindful not to set up our friends to fall into the same trap of being overly helpful that we ourselves are trying to escape.

Second, I believe that a support group provides us with a "safe place" that is unique, support that cannot be duplicated through our traditional friendships. It allows us to be with people who struggle with the same problems of codependency that we face. Being in a room with other Messiahs can be a wonderfully healing and comforting experience.

I remember my first time in such a group. It was a tremendous relief to find that other people struggled with an impossible sense of guilt and responsibility for the hurting in this world. Listening to others grieve over the years they had lost to compulsive helpaholism gave me the courage to cry my own tears. Watching others celebrate their successes gave me hope that I could also love without fear of obligation. I felt so alone in my addiction to helping. But once in a room of other Messiahs, I realized that there was hope for me too.

In addition to group support, I have found individual therapy an invaluable aid in recovery. There are several reasons why we Messiahs need a special place for honesty and safety as we move through the recovery process. We have unique needs that cannot be met through our friends, our family, or even our support group.

First, we all need a place where we can be utterly honest and feel free of any threat of punishment or exposure. Although I have friends with whom I share intimately, there are still thoughts, feelings, and experiences that I do not feel comfortable expressing. In a formal relationship with a therapist, confidentiality is to be protected. The personal and private things you tell your therapist are to remain personal and private.

Second, we need time to focus on our own needs. In a balanced, healthy friendship, both parties take turns talking and listening, leaning and supporting, giving and taking. In my recovery process, I have benefited greatly from being in a relationship in which I am not expected to do *any* of the caretaking. My part of the relationship is limited to attending my sessions and paying my fee. I am free to focus completely on myself without feeling concerned that I have "talked too long" or been too much of a burden. I am supposed to be a "burden," so to speak. That is why I am there.

As we discussed in the last session, we may overburden our friends and loved ones if we ask them to play "therapist" in our lives. Sometimes we pressure our husbands or wives to listen to us sort out issues that are actually best handled in a professional setting. We all need special attention. I have found that seeing a counselor gives me the attention I need so that I do not become overly dependent on my friends and family.

Third, even though we Messiahs tend to exude competency, under the surface is an enormous amount of pain. Many of us have suffered from serious childhood trauma. Others have been set up for the Trap through confusingly subtle, yet seriously damaging family dysfunction. We need help sorting through our memories, interpreting our dreams, and listening to our bodies to find the truth about our pain. As the tears begin to flow, we need a safe place to cry and someone to remind us that death is followed by resurrection and rebirth. When rage threatens to overwhelm us, we need someone who can help contain and direct our energy.

Sometimes the issues we face can be frightening and complex, requiring professionally trained expertise. It is important to face these difficult issues within a context designed to bring healing and resolution. A specially trained therapist can provide the safety each of us needs to face these personal and difficult issues.

If you do not have a support group or a therapist, please refer to the Recovery Skills section in this workbook for specific assistance.

Recovery Reading

The recommended reading: pages 73–77 in *When Helping You Is Hurting Me.*

Recovery Reflection

Why is asking for help so difficult?

A variety of obstacles keep us isolated from others. The first Messiah lie has convinced us that we have only ourselves upon which to rely. The second Messiah lie tells us that everyone else's needs are important, but we are being selfish if we ask for anything for ourselves.

An oversensitivity to guilt is one of the obstacles to asking for help. I believe that guilt is a positive feeling because it signals us when we have violated another human being. Healthy guilt helps us treat one another with the respect and protection that we all need. When I am caught in the Messiah Trap, however, I feel guilty about things that are not moral violations. If I walk up to you and hit you, it would be appropriate for me to feel guilty. Physically hurting you is an immoral act. But if I walk up to you and tell you that I am not available to do an errand for you as you requested, it is not appropriate for me to feel guilty. It is appropriate to feel uncomfortable when I refuse to do something you want. Feeling uncomfortable is . . . well, it's uncomfortable. While I don't especially like feeling uncomfortable, I am learning to tell the difference between guilt and discomfort.

Learning to tell the difference between guilt and discomfort can be very difficult for codependents because *our guilt meters are broken.* We feel guilty about things that are not moral violations and, believe it or not, we are often unaware when we actually hurt those in our lives. Later in this workbook we will address the damage we have done to others. Taking responsibility for our genuine moral violations is a critical part of recovery. For this session, however, I would like to concentrate on the ways that we attach guilt to actions that do not warrant such a response.

When I am caught in the Messiah Trap, I believe that there is not enough love, nurturance, time, and energy for everyone. I turn every choice into an either/or situation, with my needs pitted against yours. I act as if I have to choose between getting my needs or your needs met. I live as if we were on a lifeboat with one remaining cup of water, and must choose between giving it to you so you can survive or taking it for myself. The moral weight of such a question is tremendous! It would be very difficult if you and I were in a lifeboat, confronted with choosing which of us would die for the other. We Messiahs live as if this type of crisis, which will most likely never happen to any of us, is a normal routine.

When in the Messiah Trap, I feel as if telling you I won't do you a favor is the same as taking away your last chance for survival. It is nearly impossible for me to believe that it is possible for *both* of us to get our needs met. This may require some creativity and negotiation, but it is possible.

Exercise 1:

Oversensitivity to Guilt

I'd like you to pause for a moment and think over the past week. Were there situations in which you felt that your needs were in competition with someone else's? Did you agree to help someone, not because you wanted to, but because you felt too guilty to say no? If you took time for yourself, did guilt nag at you in the back of your mind? Or did your guilt keep you running from one obligation to another so that at the end of the week you'd taken no time for yourself at all?

A recent situation in which Carmen felt false guilt:

I felt guilty about not being able to talk to everyone at a party I had recently hosted.

A recent situation in which I felt false guilt:

When we pit our needs against the needs of others, we may feel false guilt. But when we realize that there is enough for everyone, if we are in balanced and loving relationships, then we can be free of false guilt. We no longer need to feel guilty for asking for help.

Exercise 2:   *Oversensitivity to Shame*

Guilt is felt when we have *done* something unacceptable. Shame, however, is feeling that we *are* unacceptable. Buried deep within all of us Messiahs is the fear that we are inferior. We pretend to be overly competent, overly reliable, and overly powerful because we secretly feel overly inadequate, overly worthless, and overly vulnerable. Even the thought of asking for help can bring to the surface feelings of shame and humiliation so powerful that many of us shake with fear.

It is hard for me to ask for help. I am afraid that others will view me as weak and defective. It is easy for me to feel ashamed of my vulnerability, even when my needs for support are legitimate. I believe my feelings of shame are based in the fact that I secretly look down on those who have asked me for help.

Even though many of us claim to love and respect those we help, I believe that we secretly take pride in our ability to help others. When I take care of other people, I must admit that I can feel as if I am "better" than they are. "After all, they are dependent upon me," I say quietly to myself. "They are weak but I am strong."

The two Messiah lies tell us we are, at the same time, better than everyone else and worse than everyone else. It is critical for our recovery to acknowledge that we are the *same* as everyone else. We are not any better nor are we any worse. We are human beings, made in the image of God, and therefore have no reason to be ashamed of who we are.

Describe a situation in which you asked for help and felt ashamed.

A situation in which Carmen asked for help and felt ashamed:

One night last week I became very upset and made an urgent call to my therapist. Even though he assured me that calling him was appropriate, I still felt ashamed for not being able to take care of the situation by myself.

A situation in which I asked for help and felt ashamed:

Even though asking for help may trigger feelings of guilt and shame, it is vital that we take that risk. I have never met anyone, and I have talked with a great number of Messiahs, who has escaped the Trap without asking for help.

Exercise 3: **Taking My Turn**

List all the helpful activities you did this week.

Carmen's list:

> *Visited a friend in the hospital*
> *Listened to a friend discuss her family problems*
> *Delivered groceries to a sick neighbor*
> *Helped take care of a friend's sick children*

My list:

Now, look back over the list. Did you do anything to help yourself? Probably not. It may not have occurred to you that it was good or appropriate for you to help yourself. If your name is not on this list, in reality you have done things for others before doing anything for yourself.

Now, let's think about next week. I think it is only fair that we take our turn. I recommend that you make a commitment to yourself for next week. Before you take care of anyone else, think of something you want to do for yourself and schedule time for that activity—*now.* It is time to take your turn.

Exercise 4:   ***Acknowledging That I Need Help***

We all need help because all of us are human beings. There isn't a person in the world who doesn't need support, love, under-standing, caring, and nurturance. The pain that we will face through this process of recovery can become overwhelming at times. During these darker days, we may need *extra* support and assistance. Pretending to be strong doesn't make us so. Acknowledging the truth about ourselves is much more coura-geous than pretending we feel no fear.

Describe a recent situation in which you needed help but didn't ask for assistance. Identify the reasons why you chose to deprive yourself of the help you needed.

Carmen's experience:

I was recently quite sick with the flu, and I did not have food in the house. A friend called and volunteered to bring me groceries, but I told her I did not need anything.

It is difficult for me to feel dependent. I felt guilty about being an inconvenience, and I felt ashamed about having her see me when I was so sick and weak.

My experience:

Exercise 5:   ***Acknowledging That I Deserve Help***

When I am in the Messiah Trap, I secretly believe that people who need help are inferior and weak. But as I move into recovery, I can see that the opposite is true. When I ask for help, I am actually saying, "I am a person who is worthy of time and attention. I affirm my worth by asking you to support and nurture me." One way we can increase our self-esteem is by meditating on positive affirmations. Feel free to create your own affirmation or use the one I have suggested.

Carmen's affirmation:

"I affirm my worth by asking for support and nurturance."

My affirmation:

Sit quietly with your eyes closed. Listen to your breath. Once you are in tune with your body's rhythm, meditate on the affirmation of your choice. Or try this: put on a recording of instrumental music. Dance to the rhythm and meditate on your affirmation.

Recovery Ritual

We have come to the part of our session where we create a ritual or outward expression to honor today's journey. Look back over the exercises and identify an aspect that was especially meaningful for you. Allow yourself to ponder the importance of this section for you. Create a symbol or ritual to honor yourself and your progress.

Carmen's recovery ritual:

I will take a 3 x 5 card and write in large letters: It Is My Turn. I will then tape it to my refrigerator door where I can see it every day. This will remind me to put myself on the list of people I consider worthy of my time and attention.

My recovery ritual:

Recovery Expression

Step 1:
Selecting Who to Tell About My Recovery Session

To cultivate the support and nurturance you need for today, I recommend that you contact a close friend. This may be the person you selected during your last session, or someone new.

The person Carmen will talk to about her recovery session:

A close friend

The person I will talk to about my recovery session:

Step 2:
Deciding What to Tell Others About My Recovery Session

Before you talk with this friend, I suggest that you first identify what you need from him or her. It helps me to write out what I would like to say so that I am clear about what I want to accomplish.

What Carmen will tell her friend about her recovery session:

In my session today I realized the importance of asking for support as I deal with my recovery issues. It means a great deal to me that I can talk with you about my journey.

What I will tell my friend about my recovery session:

Recovery Celebration

We have been dealing with some difficult issues today. It is now time to do something fun for ourselves. If possible, find some time today to do something you love (but rarely give yourself permission to do). Doing something simply because you enjoy it is a wonderful way to affirm your own worth. This could be

> Calling a friend who may live far away, someone you enjoy but rarely talk to nowadays
> Working a jigsaw or crossword puzzle
> Watching a favorite television show
> Window-shopping at the mall
> Cooking a favorite recipe
> Taking a nap
> Taking a quiet walk
> Putting on a favorite recording and dancing around the living room
> Spending special time with your spouse/significant other

How Carmen will affirm her worth today:

I will treat myself to a bubble bath.

How I will affirm my worth today:

Recovery Checklist

- ☐ I initiated the session with a recovery ritual
- ☐ I read pages 73–77 in *When Helping You Is Hurting Me*
- ☐ I addressed my oversensitivity to guilt
- ☐ I addressed my oversensitivity to shame
- ☐ I took my turn
- ☐ I acknowledged that I need help
- ☐ I acknowledged that I deserve help
- ☐ I created a recovery ritual
- ☐ I selected who to tell about my recovery session
- ☐ I decided what to say about my recovery session
- ☐ I celebrated my progress

 Conclude the session with your recovery ritual.

Session 3

I Am Not Alone

**Acknowledging the Need for
Spiritual Assistance**

*Initiate the session with
your recovery ritual.*

I chose the term "Messiah" to describe my addiction because I realized that I was trying to play "god" in other people's lives. I didn't trust others to run their lives with any precision. Instead, I felt it was not only my right but my duty to "help" other people. When I was finally honest with myself, I realized that my attempts to help were actually disguised efforts to control other people. Falling into the Messiah Trap, while it is an emotional and relationship problem, is fundamentally a spiritual problem. When I am a Messiah, I am pretending to be God.

Talking about God has come back into fashion these days. The term is used freely, with a wide variety of meanings. Some claim that we are all gods of our own realities. Another variation asserts that God is inside each of us. Those in Twelve-Step programs prefer to use the term "Higher Power," which can represent your personal experience of God.

I respect you and your journey and am fully expecting you and God to work out your own arrangement. At the same time, I want to be honest with you about how God has helped me through my journey. Should I share something with you that does not fit, feel free to discard it, as you no doubt have done already somewhere in this workbook.

During my years in recovery, I have experienced God as a personal presence who is always with me and loves me. When I was caught in the Messiah Trap, however, my experience was much different. Although I gave lip service to a belief in God, I lived as if God were unreliable and dangerous to me.

Recovery Reading

The recommended reading: the Twelve Steps in Appendix A of this workbook.

Recovery Reflection

The first side of the Messiah Trap insists that "If I don't do it, it won't get done," or in other words, there is no one in the world that I can depend on except myself. I didn't feel I could depend on my family, my friends, and my colleagues. Even though I was an active church member, deep in my heart I didn't believe I could depend on God either.

For me, God was irrelevant. I was surrounded by enormous pain and suffering. Overwhelmed by requests for help, I didn't feel any support or assistance from a Higher Power. I lived as if God were absent.[*]

The second side of the Messiah Trap undermined my sense of value by telling me that "Everyone else's needs take priority over mine." When I believed this lie, the best view I had of God was abusive and cruel. God was a being who watched me for any false step, driving me to perform up to an impossible standard. I was not important. In fact, I was last in line and, as far as I was spiritually concerned, God was the one who had relegated me to such a humiliating position.

I do not believe that it is possible to be caught in the Messiah Trap and at the same time have a healthy or realistic view of God. In the same way that we have been damaged emotionally and relationally by this addiction, we have suffered spiritually. I would like you to take a few moments and think about your experience of God. When you are dashing around taking care of other people, are you able to draw comfort from your faith? Or are you feeling inadequate and afraid? Is God a word with no meaning for you? Do you believe that you are loved? Or is the universe a place with a void in the center?

---

[*]See *Loving Yourself As Your Neighbor* (San Francisco: Harper & Row, 1990).

Escaping the Messiah Trap

Exercise 1:   ***Depicting My Image of God***

Draw or find a picture in a magazine or other source that depicts your mental image of God.

***Carmen's Image of God
when she is in the
Messiah Trap:***

My image of God when I am in the Messiah Trap:

The first three of the Twelve Steps are:

1. We admitted we were powerless over our addiction—
   that our lives had become unmanageable.
2. Came to believe that a Power greater than ourselves
   could restore us to sanity
3. Made a decision to turn our will and our lives over to the
   care of God as we understood God.

I remember first hearing these words in a support group but feeling unable to relate to them. The pain was too real, the disappointment too fresh for me to trust anyone, let alone a God I couldn't see, touch, or feel. I was too full of rage to have any room for hope. But I did know what it felt like to be powerless. My life had most certainly become unmanageable. Now that I couldn't depend on myself anymore, to whom could I turn?

During those dark and difficult days, I learned a very important truth. All my life I had tried to be "good" for God, as a way to earn my worth. I lived in constant fear that if I made a mistake, God would condemn and punish me. And yet, week after week, as I listened to the other members of my support group talk about their mistakes, their failures, and their successes, I realized that God was not in the business of punishing us, but of loving us. It was more important for me to be honest with God than to pretend to be good.

And so I took a chance. I sat down one afternoon and told God exactly what I thought of things. I spewed rage and resentment that had been bottled up for years. A river of tears ran down my cheeks, tears of sadness, disappointment, and confusion. "Where were you when I needed help?" I asked. "Why do you demand so much from me? When will I ever feel peace?"

No lightning flashed. No thunder rolled. But my life took on a new direction from that day on. I had finally been honest with myself and my God. I opened myself spiritually in much the same way I had emotionally when I dared to join the support group or started therapy. Like others who have experienced healing through a spiritual path, I was beginning to admit that I needed help from Someone more powerful than me. And maybe, just maybe, that Someone could and would help me.

Exercise 2: **_Identifying Feelings I Associate with God_**

Please check:

☐	Anger	☐	Hope
☐	Satisfaction	☐	Fear
☐	Frustration	☐	Anxiety
☐	Guidance	☐	Love
☐	Guilt	☐	Shame
☐	Abandonment	☐	Longing
☐	Rejection	☐	Acceptance
☐	Safety	☐	Criticism
☐	Understanding	☐	Compassion
☐	Disappointment	☐	Peace
☐	Distress	☐	Grief
☐	Joy	☐	Apathy
☐	_____	☐	_____
☐	_____	☐	_____

You may want to describe more fully the feelings and thoughts you are having. If so, please use this space:

Exercise 3: **_Identifying the Obstacles to Trusting God_**

I resisted turning my life over to the care of God. There were a number of obstacles standing in the way of such trust. Even though I desperately needed help, I had trouble asking God for assistance. I urge you to explore deeply and to identify what may be keeping you from asking for the spiritual help you need.

Do you believe that a Power greater than yourself is available to restore your life to sanity?

If not, what are the obstacles standing in your way?

The obstacles standing in Carmen's way of trusting her Higher Power:

I am afraid that God expects me to help everybody I meet and will be disappointed in me if I fail. When I am in trouble I am not sure I can count on God.

The obstacles standing in my way of trusting my Higher Power:

Exercise 4:   *Asking God for Help*

You and I know that this world is very confusing. We have tried our best to change the world and it is still in a mess. Not only have I had to admit that I can't change the world, I am repeatedly faced with the reality that I can't even change myself.

Honesty is the first step toward healing. As we are honest with God, spiritual healing begins.

I believe that the love and healing I have experienced during my years in recovery find their source in a God who knows and loves me. I rely on that power every day, every hour. I do not consider myself a theological master or a spiritual guru. My prayer is simple. My prayer is this—*Help!*

I encourage you to turn your life over to God, as honestly as you can.

Carmen's prayer:

Help! I try to be the best person I know how to be. But the more I try to do the right thing, the more things come apart. Now I have to face the fact that my life is out of control. I am addicted to a compulsive, codependent lifestyle that is ruining my health and destroying my relationships. Please help restore my life to sanity. I turn my life over to your care.

My prayer:

Recovery Ritual

In the preceding sessions, I have challenged you to ask for help—again and again. First, I asked you to trust me and follow the exercises outlined in this workbook. Then I urged you to talk with selected friends and family, asking them for support and understanding. The next challenge was to find a support group and ask for help in a public arena. And then, for the deeply private parts of your recovery, you were encouraged to ask a therapist for assistance.

Today, the challenge is on a spiritual level—to ask God for help. This moment is a sacred one, deserving of honor. You have shown great courage in asking for help.

For the next few moments, allow your imagination to create a special ritual to honor your session today. You have released control of that over which you have had no real control. You have opened yourself up to a deeper source of strength.

Carmen's recovery ritual:

I will write my full name on a piece of paper and place it in my fireplace. I will light the paper. The ascending smoke will symbolize my decision to depend on God.

My recovery ritual:

Recovery Expression

Our spirituality is perhaps the most private part of our lives. Although some people are quite verbal about their faith, I find that I am careful with whom I share. This session, more than any other, is the most private for me. That is one reason I placed it in the middle of the workbook and not at the beginning. I have felt comfortable sharing with you today because I believe that only people who take their recovery seriously will ever read this far in the workbook. If you have made the effort to come to this point, you are most likely someone I can trust with my vulnerability.

During this part of the session, I encourage you to contact someone you trust and share what you have learned. Choose someone with whom you feel comfortable, perhaps your therapist, a spiritual director, a rabbi, a pastor, or a very dear friend. Please tell them about your session today. Some of you may even feel comfortable sharing this with your support group.

If you are like me, a little private about spiritual issues, I want you to feel free to share, not with another human being, but directly with your Higher Power. After all, God is now a viable part of your recovery support system.

Step 1:
Deciding Who to Tell About My Recovery Session

The person Carmen will talk to about her recovery session:

My therapist

The person I will talk to about my recovery session:

Step 2:
Deciding What to Tell Others About My Recovery Session

What Carmen will say about her recovery session:

I feel an enormous burden has been lifted from my shoulders because during my recovery session I realized it was not my responsibility to play God. I acknowledge that I need help and I am learning to trust that God is there to help me.

What I will say about my recovery session:

Recovery Celebration

Since we have focused on the spiritual aspect of life in our session, I think it would be a good balance to focus our celebration on our bodies. Sit quietly for a moment and allow yourself to become aware of your body. How is your body feeling at this moment? Are you feeling tension in any part of your body? Are you hungry? sleepy? excited?

As you ponder how you can celebrate today's session, I encourage you to find something that nurtures your body as well as your spirit. Perhaps it is time to look in the yellow pages and find a local bodywork center. I receive a massage from a professional massage therapist every week as a way to honor myself spiritually and physically. This is a very nurturing part of my recovery process.

If a professional massage is not available to you, perhaps you could ask a friend or loved one to give you a back massage. This is a wonderful way to celebrate your progress today.

If a massage does not meet your needs, feel free to create another way of celebrating your session. If possible, find a way to honor yourself spiritually and physically. You deserve a grand reward for your progress today!

Recovery Checklist

- ☐ I initiated the session with a recovery ritual
- ☐ I read the Twelve Steps
- ☐ I depicted my image of God
- ☐ I identified feelings I associate with God
- ☐ I identified obstacles to trusting God
- ☐ I asked God for help
- ☐ I created a recovery ritual
- ☐ I selected who to tell about my recovery session
- ☐ I decided what to say about my recovery session
- ☐ I celebrated my progress

 Conclude the session with your recovery ritual.

Session 4

I Am Important

Learning to Cooperate with the Process of Growth, Part I

I believe the process of growth involves two steps: (1) letting go of the past and (2) embracing a new future. Many of us fear letting go in any form because, deep in our hearts, we do not trust that rebirth will follow. We have been damaged spiritually by the Messiah Trap and have lost faith in God's promise of rebirth and renewal.

When we are in the Messiah Trap, we are unable to experience rebirth. Our addiction promises us happiness but never delivers. Instead, our lives are used up, burned out, and wasted on ineffective suffering. My heart breaks when I look back over the years I threw away on codependency. Those years are dead to me and forever gone. I sacrificed everything, deceived by the illusion that I would be appreciated and loved through compulsive helping. But I was deeply disappointed. When we are in dysfunctional relationships, rebirth never follows the losses. We suffer but have nothing to show in the end for our sacrifice.

When we move out of our addiction, however, and learn to cooperate with the process of healing and growth, loss is not the end. As illustrated in the story of Jesus, death is not the last chapter but rather rebirth and renewal. One way we can discern whether we are cooperating with the process of growth is to assess whether our suffering results in healing, our losses make way for new loves, and our confusion gives birth to clear insight.

During this and the next session, we are going to explore both aspects of the process of growth—letting go of the past and embracing a new future. The exercises will focus on letting go of our attempts to earn our worth. Instead, we will embrace our intrinsic value, grounded in the fact that we are already acceptable and lovable. Instead of pretending we are perfect, we will focus on letting go of our Messiah masks. We will embrace our common humanity and acknowledge our needs. Last, we will identify some of the ways we Messiahs sabotage our healing by trying to control rather than cooperate with this natural rhythm of letting go of the old and embracing the new.

Recovery Reading

The recommended reading: pages 29–35 in *When Helping You Is Hurting Me.*

Recovery Reflection

The reading for today covers four Messiah characteristics—all behaviors that keep us from cooperating with the process of growth. A Messiah is someone who

1. Tries to earn a sense of worth by acting worthy
2. Lets others determine his or her actions
3. Needs to overachieve
4. Is attracted to helping those with similar pain

In contrast, a person in recovery participates in both aspects of the process of growth. A person in recovery is genuinely helpful, someone I call the "Healthy Helper." A Healthy Helper is someone who

1. Acknowledges dependence upon God and embraces his or her intrinsic self-worth
2. Is able to address personal pain directly and takes responsibility for his or her choices
3. Is able to set realistic goals and limits
4. Is able to empathize with others and help in effective ways; does not become enmeshed or overly involved

The Messiah approach does not lead to rebirth. Instead, our addiction leads us to a premature death in forms such as burnout, emotional distress, physical illness, marital problems, and, perhaps for some, premature physical death. Like all addictions, codependency binds us to a dead end with no renewal.

In contrast, the process of growth incorporates letting go of the past as a natural step toward embracing a new future. The Healthy Helper is one who is open, flexible, and creative. Relationships become a source of support, not merely more obligation. While there is time for grief and facing the pain, there is also plenty of time for celebration and enjoyment. So how do we discard our Messiah approach to life and embrace that of the Healthy Helper? Since suffering, pain, and loss cannot be avoided, how do we cooperate with the process to include renewal in the rhythm of our lives?

Exercise 1: **Identifying Ways I Try to Earn My Worth by Acting Worthy**

We Messiahs secretly feel inferior to others. Driven by low self-esteem, we dedicate all our energy and talents to one goal— earning a sense of worth and well-being. We pretend to be stronger, wiser, calmer, kinder, and more reliable than we genuinely believe ourselves to be.

Check the ways you may compensate for feelings of low self-esteem:

☐ Acting "nice"	☐ Hiding fears
☐ Acting competent	☐ Compulsive overeating
☐ Compulsive dieting	☐ Hiding feelings of
☐ Pretending to be strong	loneliness
☐ Acting out sexually	☐ Compulsive celibacy
☐ Feeling guilty when saying no	☐ Hiding feelings of anger
☐ Working excessive hours	☐ Fearing intimacy
☐ Feeling better than others	☐ Feeling inferior to others
☐ Overachieving	☐ _____
☐ _____	☐ _____

Accepting the degree to which we compensate for our low self-esteem is often difficult. An even more difficult challenge can be letting go of these familiar patterns of self-protection. Visualization is one of the ways that I "let go" of the past and of self-defeating emotional patterns. I imagine wrapping up an old, self-defeating behavior or situation in a large cloth. Then, I imagine tying this burden onto a large balloon. As I release my past, this balloon rises to God. I am then free to embrace my new future, unencumbered with past baggage. Feel free to use this visualization as you learn to let go of the past, or create your own process of "letting go." Whatever method you choose to use, I urge you to let go of the futile attempt to compensate for feelings of low self-esteem. As you release these behaviors, the way will be cleared for a deeper, more satisfying self-love and more authentic, loving relationships with others.

Exercise 2:   *Acknowledging Dependence on God and Embracing My Self-Worth*

As we release our grip on old ways of earning our worth, our hands are freed to embrace our authentic value. I believe that positive self-esteem is rooted in a positive relationship with my God. As I trust that I am loved and valued by a Higher Power, I am freed from the drive to prove myself.

In a moment we will begin an exercise of visualization that acknowledges our dependence on God and helps us to embrace our self-worth. Visualization is a process whereby we interact with our own private world of symbols and feelings. Symbols have been the language of dreams and the imagination for centuries. In the Bible Moses encountered God in the symbol of the burning bush; Peter, a disciple of Jesus, had a dream in which God spoke to him through the symbols of the sheet and the cornucopia. These are but two examples of how symbols can communicate personal truth and direction. We all have symbols that carry special meaning for us. This exercise will help you access your feelings about God and your self-worth in the symbols that speak directly to you.

Sit quietly for a moment and clear your mind. Visualize yourself in a place of complete safety. You may feel the most secure in the mountains by a stream, on a sandy beach, in the middle of a secluded desert, or beside a tropical waterfall. Take time to create this place for yourself so that each detail is pleasing and comforting to you.

After you feel at home in your special place, visualize your Higher Power coming to you. For some of you, the symbol of your Higher Power may appear in the form of an animal such as a dove, a lion, or an eagle. For others, God may take the form of light or fire or water. God has also been visualized in human forms, such as a grandfather or a comforting mother. For me, a very powerful symbol of God comes to me in the form of Jesus.

After your Higher Power has joined you in your special place, ask for a gift. Imagine your Higher Power responding to your request. Accept the gift offered. Examine the gift. Enjoy the gift. Explore how this gift can assist you in your journey.

When you are ready, begin to return to the present. Remember, you can return to this safe and sacred place anytime you need assurance, guidance, or love from your Higher Power. As your mind leaves your special place, embrace your value by focusing on the following meditation:

I am loved and valued.

Exercise 3:   *Identifying How I Let Others Determine My Actions*

When I try to earn my worth, I immediately give up control over my own life. I give other people power over me because I give them power over my sense of worth and well-being. Since others decide if I am acceptable or unacceptable, lovable or unlovable, I can become desperate to get other people's approval. When in the Messiah Trap, I live for that glimmer in someone's eye that tells me I am needed. I have lived to hear someone say, "Carmen, you are wonderful to me. I couldn't have gotten through this without you." For that brief moment, I felt good about myself. But as soon as that person moved on, my haunting self-doubts returned.

Think back over the past week and identify a situation in which you gave another person power over your sense of self-worth and, therefore, over your choices and behavior.

A situation in which Carmen let someone else determine her actions:

I received a phone call from a local charity organization asking for a donation. I had already sent off support checks to the organizations I had selected to support this month. Even though the money budgeted for donations had been spent, I felt guilty about saying no to this new request. I didn't want to appear insensitive or uncaring. So, instead of keeping to my budget, I buckled to the pressure and made a substantial pledge. It was more important for me to have the caller's approval than to be responsible to my financial plan.

A situation in which I let someone else determine my actions:

Sit for a moment and ponder this situation. Visualize wrapping this experience in a large sheet. Imagine tying this cloth to a balloon and then sending it to God. Let go of this situation and, with it, the willingness to let other people determine your actions.

Exercise 4:   *Learning to Take Responsibility for My Own Choices*

If I allow others to control my behavior, I am not free to cooperate with the process of growth. Instead of listening to my inner voice, I am straining my ears to hear words of approval from those around me. Instead of cooperating with the guidance I receive from God, I am doing whatever I think may please someone else. My attention is not on the process of growth; rather it is on my addictive need for approval.

Instead of allowing others to control my life, it is critical that I learn to take responsibility for my own behavior and actions. Instead of trying to manipulate other people into telling me what a wonderful person I am, I must focus my attention on loving and attending to myself.

Look back at the previous exercise. Pretend you could relive that experience, this time as someone who is secure in a sense of self-worth. Visualize the balloon descending with a special gift of self-worth. See yourself as someone with nothing to prove, free to choose among a variety of options. As you embrace the gift of love and security, imagine how you would respond differently to this situation. How would you have felt? Stronger? More creative? More loving? Less vulnerable? Now, replay the situation in your mind and, instead of giving someone else control over your actions, take responsibility for yourself and make your own choices. Embrace a new way of interacting with other people, a way of love and caring, not obligation or control.

Carmen's visualization:

If I had felt secure in my worth and acceptability, I would have responded differently to the caller asking for a donation. I would have listened to the description of the organization to determine if this was a group I wanted to support in the future. My self-esteem would have allowed me to assess my genuine interest in supporting this service, rather than impulsively making a pledge to get approval from the caller. If this was not a group I wanted to support, I would have politely declined.

If I found that this was a service I wanted to support, I would explain that, while at the moment I was supporting other worthy causes, I would be interested in discussing future support. I could then readjust my budget so that I could wisely and thoughtfully allocate my resources in the future.

My visualization:

Exercise 5:   ***Identifying My Need to Overachieve***

Those of us in the Messiah Trap have been rewarded all our lives for being overly responsible. When we were children, many of us were complimented for being "good," "mature," and "helpful" boys and girls.

In the past several years I have traveled all over the United States leading workshops on how to escape the Messiah Trap. This has given me the opportunity to meet many people who claim to have fallen into the Messiah Trap. I have been struck by the fact that the Messiahs I have met are all exceptionally talented, energetic, and caring people. These are not incompetent people. To the contrary, the people I have met have been high achievers, usually well educated, and certainly successful in whatever area they have chosen. We Messiahs are usually committed, enthusiastic, and extremely talented.

It breaks my heart to realize that our talents and energy are being wasted and misdirected by our codependency. Instead of feeling good about what we achieve, we feel driven to *over-achieve*. If someone referred to me as average, I would consider that an insult. To me, being labeled as average is the same as being called a failure. As a Messiah, it is not acceptable to achieve at pace with my age; I need to be "above" the others.

This sets me up for black-and-white thinking so that everything I do is either good or bad, perfect or a failure. We Messiahs become perfectionistic and unrealistically critical of ourselves. Instead of being free to develop my talents at my own pace, the Messiah Trap drives me to focus my energy into my addiction.

Identify one way in which you are perfectionistic or overachieving. Some Messiahs work excessive hours. Others become perfectionistic so that whatever they do must meet impossible standards. Be as specific as you can.

One way Carmen is perfectionistic and overachieving:

After I make a presentation, I look over the evaluation forms. If I am feeling good about myself, I am able to receive criticism constructively and make changes that are helpful. But if I am doubting my worth and am falling back into the Messiah Trap, any criticism cuts me to the quick. I may get high ratings from most attendees but feel like a failure if one person rates me negatively. If I do not receive a perfect rating, I can feel like a total failure.

One way I am perfectionistic and overachieving:

By using the balloon visualization or your own method, let go of this experience and, with it, the drive toward perfectionism. Instead of attempting to be perfect, open yourself up to being human, lovable, just the way you are.

| Exercise 6: | ### *Setting Realistic Expectations for Myself* |

As I let go of the futile trap of earning self-worth, I am given the opportunity to set new and realistic goals for myself. I am free, at last, to invest myself in activities that I want to do. Instead of feeling obligated to people out of guilt, I can develop relationships with people I actually care about and enjoy! No longer are we compelled to do whatever others demand. We can spend our time in whatever manner we choose.

Review the last exercise, where we described a situation in which we overextended ourselves. Think about this situation and identify how you can put more realistic boundaries on this activity or relationship. Write out specific limits you would like to set. Embrace a new future by visualizing yourself repeating this experience, but this time set realistic limits on your time and energy.

Carmen's visualization:

Rather than fool myself into thinking that it is possible to give the "perfect" presentation, I would like to hold onto a more realistic standard of assessing my performance.

1. I will listen to my own feelings and experience of the presentation. If I enjoy the presentation and honestly share myself, I will consider the experience to be successful. If I feel off-balance or identify areas that could be improved, I will set out ways to strengthen my skill. But I will know that no interaction is "perfect."

2. I will receive the written and verbal assessments of the presentation as helpful suggestions, not bottom-line, definitive, or authoritative truth. As I accept that I am always learning and growing, these suggestions can help point me in new directions.

3. If I receive an especially negative reaction from someone, I will take this experience to my support group, therapist, or friend. In a safe place, I can be free to explore my part in triggering such a negative reaction. With support, I can discern what can be discarded and what can be taken in as helpful information. I need never, however, give up my sense of well-being, because I do not have to be perfect to feel good about myself.

My visualization:

Exercise 7:   **Identifying How Those I Help Reflect My Own Pain**

Since childhood, we Messiahs have been taught to ignore our own legitimate needs and attend instead to the needs of others. As adults, we simply do not have the skills to identify or address our own needs. Many of us take this a step further and pretend that we have no needs or desires. Buried deep within our unconscious minds are memories and pain that we are yet unprepared to face.

Hiding our needs does not eliminate them, however. We still have needs and desires whether we admit them to ourselves or not. Instead of facing our pain directly, we Messiahs find ourselves unconsciously attracted to people who share our hurts, wishes, and needs.

To explore this characteristic, make a list of the last five people you have helped. Then, to the right of each name, write down what you did for that person.

Carmen's list:

1. *Friend—listened as she discussed struggles with the new man in her life*
2. *Neighbor—listened as she discussed her recent illness*
3. *Friend—visited him in the hospital after surgery*
4. *Colleague—listened as he complained about his boss*
5. *Friend—helped her decide which therapist to see*

My list:

1.

2.

3.

4.

5.

Exercise 8: **Identifying My Own Needs and Wants**

As I look over my list, I realize that I have given to others what I have needed for myself. This is a common experience for

Messiahs. We are attracted to people with similar needs and we often give to them what we want for ourselves. Review your list for a moment and see if you also have given to others what you need for yourself. Describe the needs that seem to be especially relevant for you today.

Carmen's needs:

I listen to other people and attend to their need for attention. I can see that I also need to have people listen to me when I talk about my feelings. I need attention and help sorting out what decisions to make.

My needs:

Visualize tying the pretense that you have no legitimate needs onto a balloon. Release the balloon to God. Wait a few moments and allow God to send the balloon back to you, filled with the needs you identified in this exercise. Take each need, one by one, and hold that need close to your heart. Embrace each need and commit yourself to taking responsibility for attending to your needs in a loving and compassionate manner.

Recovery Ritual

During today's session, we began to cooperate with the process of growth. We let go of old passions and opened the door to rebirth and renewal. We turned our attention from earning our worth by acting worthy to embracing our worth and honoring our legitimate needs for healing and growth. Instead of pretending we have no needs or desires, we had courage to be vulnerable in a new way.

Look over the list you have developed that identifies what you need. This is a special list, one that deserves respect. It takes courage to acknowledge what you need. I suggest that you develop a recovery ritual that symbolizes the courage you illustrated today. You may want to develop a ritual that reflects the theme of letting go of the past and embracing renewal.

Carmen's recovery ritual:

I will play instrumental music that is positive and joyful. I will use dance as a symbolic ritual. I will use movement to commemorate the cycle of letting go and embracing renewal. As I dance, I will express my acceptance of my worth and my legitimate needs.

My recovery ritual:

Recovery Expression

Step 1:
Selecting Who to Tell About My Recovery Session

Select someone you believe has the same kind of courage you have illustrated today. This person may be a friend, family member, therapist, or group member—anyone who is cooperating with the process of growth.

The person Carmen will talk to about her recovery session:

Friend

The person I will talk to about my recovery session:

Step 2:
Deciding What to Tell Others About My Recovery Session

As you share with the person you have selected, I would like you to stay aware of your own feelings. Watch for any longing you may have for *approval*. It is appropriate and helpful to receive support from others. It is a step backward, however, if we allow ourselves to remain dependent upon the approval of others.

As you think over what you want to say, you may decide to explain how you are learning to trust God and the promise of renewal. Instead of allowing others to determine your actions, you are taking more responsibility for your own choices. Your need to overachieve is dying, replaced by realistic and loving expectations for yourself. Instead of being unconsciously drawn to those who reflect your own pain, you are learning to clearly and consciously identify what you need and desire.

What Carmen will say about her recovery session:

I am learning about letting go of my old way of doing things, which left me shortchanged and drained. As I let go, I am freeing myself to new opportunities. In the session today I was able to identify my need to have attention and for others to listen to me. It is especially important to me that you are my friend and willing to listen to me today. I need your support.

Recovery Celebration

Learning to cooperate with the process of growth can be a daring and exciting adventure. I recommend that the celebration you develop today be one that is enjoyable and fun. Make an opportunity to enjoy something that you usually don't give yourself permission to experience. This could be riding a carousel, taking a stroll along the beach or through the woods, or receiving a professional massage.

Review the list you made of your needs and desires. Select one of the items on that list and turn your need into a goal. Develop a plan of action to achieve that goal. If you have trouble finding a way to meet your need, you may want to pretend that you are trying to reach this goal on behalf of someone else. We Messiahs can be extremely creative when we are helping someone else and yet forget all our skills when it comes to meeting our own needs. Celebrate today's session by giving yourself something you legitimately need. And don't forget . . . *enjoy yourself along the way!*

Recovery Checklist

- ☐ I initiated the session with a recovery ritual
- ☐ I read pages 29–35 in *When Helping You Is Hurting Me*
- ☐ I identified ways I try to earn my worth by acting worthy
- ☐ I learned to embrace my God-given value
- ☐ I identified how I let others determine my actions
- ☐ I learned new ways to take responsibility for my actions
- ☐ I identified my need to overachieve
- ☐ I set realistic expectations for myself
- ☐ I identified some of my own needs and desires
- ☐ I created a recovery ritual
- ☐ I selected who to tell about my recovery session
- ☐ I decided what to say about my recovery session
- ☐ I celebrated my progress

Conclude the session with your recovery ritual.

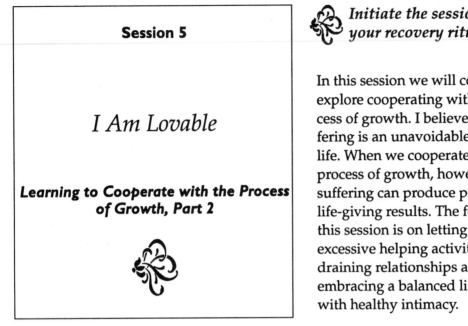

Session 5

I Am Lovable

Learning to Cooperate with the Process of Growth, Part 2

Initiate the session with your recovery ritual.

In this session we will continue to explore cooperating with the process of growth. I believe that suffering is an unavoidable part of life. When we cooperate with the process of growth, however, our suffering can produce positive and life-giving results. The focus of this session is on letting go of excessive helping activities and draining relationships and then embracing a balanced lifestyle with healthy intimacy.

Recovery Reading

The recommended reading: pages 36–40 in *When Helping You Is Hurting Me.*

Recovery Reflection

As described in the reading, a Messiah exhibits characteristics that lead to death, not renewal. A Messiah is one who

1. Experiences difficulty in establishing peer and intimate relationships
2. Is caught in a cycle of isolation
3. Is driven to endless activity
4. Stops when he or she drops

In contrast, a Healthy Helper is one who

1. Is able to establish peer and intimate relationships
2. Is able to belong to the group while retaining a sense of self

3. Takes satisfaction in a job well done and is able to relax and play

4. Is able to solve problems effectively; cooperates with the process of death and resurrection so that growth and healing can occur

Exercise 1:   *Identifying Difficulties I Have in My Peer and Intimate Relationships*

Many of us Messiahs are with people all day long and yet are achingly lonely. Our lives are filled with activity, but we experience little satisfaction or pleasure. Consciously, I have always wanted positive and satisfying relationships. My family, friends, and romantic relationships have not always provided me with the safety, nurturance, and excitement I have desired, however. In fact, these relationship have been the source of a great deal of disappointment and hurt.

As I honestly assess my relationships, I realize that I unknowingly sabotage intimacy in a variety of ways. Intimacy, whether it be with a family member, friend, or lover, is a spontaneous creation that is born through the participation of both parties. Such creativity requires time, energy, and flexibility. When in the Messiah Trap, I do not have the time for intimacy (I am busy taking care of everyone else), I do not have the energy (I am exhausted by the demands), and I certainly don't have flexibility (I am driven by my inner needs for approval).

Another way I sabotage my attempts at intimacy is by selecting people who are not capable of healthy interactions. When in the Messiah Trap, I tend to choose people who need me, not people who are ready and willing to love me as I really am. Instead of enjoying my time with friends and romantic interests, I focus on helping them in some way.

A third way I sabotage myself is by allowing my fear of intimacy to keep me imprisoned. I hide behind my Messiah role and never risk telling people who I am. It is much easier for me to pretend to be in control, to be perfect. Risking honesty and allowing anyone to find out my weaknesses and fears is just too frightening to me. So, I pass up many chances for intimacy.

These are several ways the Messiah Trap has kept me from experiencing intimacy. Can you identify ways you have sabotaged yourself?

Describe a situation in which you denied yourself an opportunity for intimacy.

Difficulties Carmen has had in establishing intimate relationships:

A friend who lives in another state came through Los Angeles on business. He called to see if we could get together. I had filled my schedule so tightly that I had no flexibility to see him. I regret missing that opportunity for deepening our relationship.

Difficulties I have had in establishing peer and intimate relationships:

Exercise 2: **Developing the Ability to Establish Peer and Intimate Relationships**

In order for me to establish healthier peer and intimate relationships, I have had to confront my need to make a place for intimacy to occur. When I am in the Messiah Trap, there is no room in my life for anything but obligation and busyness.

Escaping the Messiah Trap

I have needed to make room for intimacy in several ways. The first involves what I call the "pruning" part of recovery. Pruning is a critical recovery skill, one that can be temporarily painful yet ultimately produce great joy and satisfaction. A friend of mine told me about visiting his grandparents and, in their backyard, finding his favorite lemon tree withered and near death. Most of the branches were cracked and gnarled, with the deadwood spreading down into the trunk. Taking a saw and ax to his beloved tree, he cut off every dead branch. When he finally stood back to see what was left, instead of a large lemon tree only a stubby trunk and one branch remained. It was a sad and ugly sight.

Some time later, my friend returned to visit his grandparents and to see what had come of his attempt to save the lemon tree. The lemon tree, though growing in a different direction than before, was alive, healthy, and full of plump fruit. Those of us in recovery also need to prune away the dead branches of our lives so that new fruit can be born.

Sometimes, like the lemon tree, our lives are so filled with underbrush and deadwood that we are in danger of burnout, and even death. When I had my serious burnout experience in 1985, much of my life was consumed by my addiction to helping. Pruning for me then meant changing my employment, moving from where I was living, cutting off many relationships, and altering my personal life. I needed radical pruning.

Since then, however, the pruning in my life has been a branch here, a branch there. Sometimes I take on too many projects and then realize I must cut back. At other times a relationship may become too demanding or out of balance and adjustments need to be made. In serious cases, the relationship is severed. But most of the time, pruning comes more in the form of setting firmer limits on my time or nurturance.

As Messiahs, we can fill our lives with too many people. But as we let go of the past and embrace renewal, we will see a positive pattern occur in our peer and intimate relationships. The first part of the process is letting go. Those relationships that are not conducive to our recovery tend to die off. Some of these losses can be extremely painful while the exit of others, quite frankly, can be an enormous relief. Those parts of our lives, whether they be relationships, habits, desires, or characteristics, are pruned away in the same way that a plant is cut back to make way for new blooms.

The pruning part of recovery, with its grief and sadness, is a time when we are asked to hold onto our faith in the process of growth. It is easy for me to be so aware of my losses that I lose hope in rebirth. People leave me and I fear that I will always be alone. But I have found in my recovery journey, again and again, that winter is followed by spring. Once I let go of those relationships that are no longer supportive to my recovery, new and more supportive relationships enter my life.

Second, I have needed to make room for intimacy by restructuring my priorities. In order to cultivate healthy intimacy, I have needed to make more time, invest more energy, and become more flexible. I can't get off the hook by merely taking care of others. My healthy and intimate relationships have expected more healthy intimacy from me. These friends are not content to be scheduled in between meetings. Instead, a full commitment to the relationship has been expected. I am expected to share myself and my feelings, not merely act the role of a helper.

In the next exercise you will find a drawing of a tree. I would like you to write on each tree branch various relationships and activities with which you are currently involved. Take some time to assess these various relationships and activities. Color those relationships that are balanced and those activities that are life-giving a light brown. Color those relationships that are draining and those activities that are excessive a light gray. Take a black marker and draw where the branches should be pruned back. After you identify the areas that need to be pruned, make a commitment to yourself to let go of these unhelpful responsibilities.

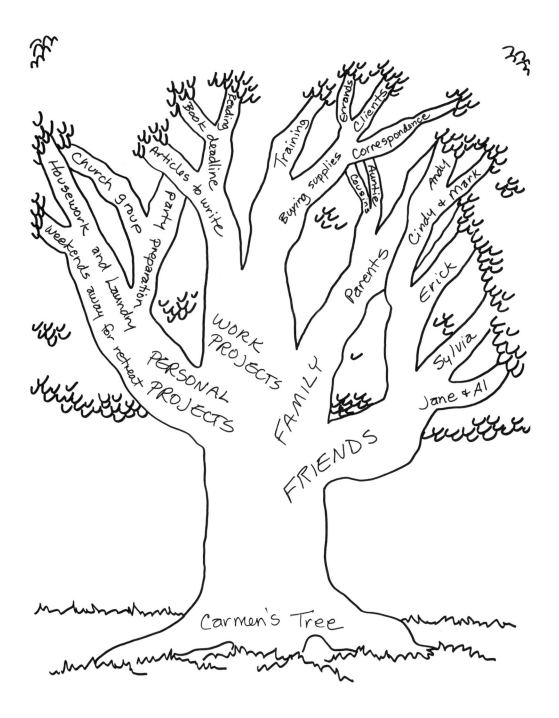

Carmen's Tree

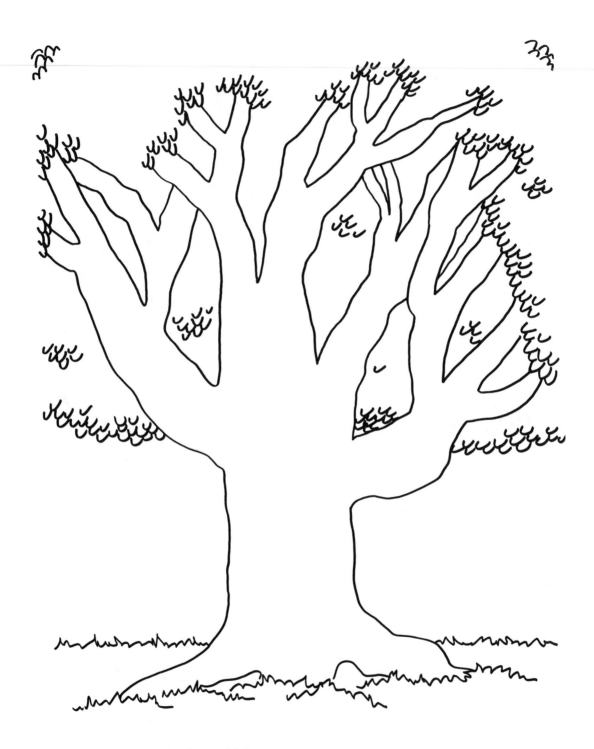

Escaping the Messiah Trap

Exercise 3:   *Identifying Ways I Am Caught in a Cycle of Isolation*

Because we are not able to cultivate and enjoy intimate relation-ships, we Messiahs experience intense loneliness. This type of loneliness has been very confusing to me. I can be with people all day and yet feel terribly alone. I remember sitting in a com-mittee meeting and watching my friends and colleagues excit-edly engaged in discussion. From the enthusiastic looks on their faces, it appeared to me that their lives were working out fine. So what was wrong with me? Why was I so miserable? Here I was committed to making the world a better place. Why was my world such a dreary place?

I felt embarrassed to talk about my feelings of loneliness. I was afraid to let anyone know that I had problems or concerns. Instead of drawing comfort from my association with friends and colleagues, I felt odd, weird, and inadequate. This, of course, only served to confirm my worst fear—that I really was a worthless person.

This is how the cycle of isolation works: We feel bad about ourselves and so we try to earn our worth by acting worthy. When this doesn't work (and, of course, it never does), we feel even more inadequate and flawed. Our low self-esteem, which has now been intensified rather than alleviated, drives us even harder to hide our true selves. Deeper and deeper we go into a prison of loneliness, convinced that no one could love us.

Draw a picture of yourself when you are busy taking care of other people and yet feel lonely. Include as many people as you like. Around the edge of the picture, write the feelings you have while you are with these people.

Carmen's drawing:

My drawing:

Escaping the Messiah Trap

Exercise 4: ***Learning to Belong to a Group While Retaining a Sense of Self***

Instead of a downward cycle of isolation, those of us in recovery experience an upward spiral of renewal and rebirth of self-esteem. As we embrace our own worth, we naturally draw people into our lives who are more able to treat us with respect. The more we risk honestly sharing ourselves and finding ourselves accepted and nurtured, the better we feel about ourselves. The better we feel about ourselves, the more courage we have to share who we really are. Instead of seeing another person as yet another drain on our energy, we can experience a more balanced sense of nurturance and joy.

A Healthy Helper is able to be a part of a group, whether it be professional or personal, and draw nurturance. The Messiah, however, rarely experiences a group as nurturing. The Messiah is too busy trying to please everyone to receive anything for him- or herself. And yet, strangely enough, the Healthy Helper is not as dependent upon the group as is the Messiah. When I am confident of my worth, I am free to enjoy those in the group, no longer needing their approval to participate. When I am caught in the Messiah Trap, I am too afraid to say how I really feel since the threat of rejection is overwhelming.

Draw a picture of yourself when you are with people you love and enjoy. Include as many people as you like. Around the edge of the picture, write the feelings you have while you are with these people.

Carmen's drawing:

My drawing:

Escaping the Messiah Trap

Exercise 5:   ***Assessing My Drive for Endless Activity***

We Messiahs are driving frantically down a road of activity that has no end. How many people will we have to help before we believe we are good people? How many sacrifices do we have to make before we believe we can take our turn? How many hours do we have to work until we believe we deserve to relax and play?

Looking at what we give to others can be a real eye-opener. Take out your calendar and realistically count up how many hours you spent this week on helping activities. Then add up how much time you spent on taking care of yourself. How much time have you spent doing fun things? It can be sobering to see, in black and white, how endless our obligations can be—with no time for ourselves.

Carmen's calendar:

_42_ *Hours spent on helping activities*
_7_ *Hours spent on myself, fun, or cultivating intimacy*

My calendar:

_____ Hours spent on helping activities
_____ Hours spent on myself, fun, or cultivating intimacy

Exercise 6:   ***Learning to Take Satisfaction in a Job Well Done;***
Relaxing and Playing

In contrast to the endless activity generated by the Messiah Trap, the Healthy Helper can relax, celebrate, and play. One reason that the Healthy Helper is able to take satisfaction in a job well done is that a person in recovery knows *when* the job is done! Because the Healthy Helper knows how to set realistic goals, each task has an end point that can be realistically achieved.

Celebration is an activity that has no place for those of us caught in the Messiah Trap. It is so important for our recovery, however, that I included celebration as a regular part of every session in this workbook. Celebration is a part of the rebirth cycle of the process of growth. Take out your calendar again and schedule a special time of celebration and fun. Ask at least one other person to join you . . . make it a party!

Carmen's celebration:

I will ask two of my friends to go to the local comedy club on Friday night. I love to laugh, and this is a great way to celebrate the positive yet hard work I have done in recovery.

My celebration:

Exercise 7:   ***Identifying How My Addiction Will Lead Me to Burnout***

It is easier, perhaps, to see how certain addictions can be deadly. Alcohol addiction can destroy a person's liver, resulting in premature death. Drug addiction can damage the brain and other organs. A drug overdose can result in immediate death. But other addictions, such as ours, seem to be harmless or even beneficial.

But don't be deceived. The Messiah Trap is relentless in its demands on those in its grip. It demands that we give everything for nothing in return. Total loyalty is required. We

Messiahs are not to believe anything but what our addiction promises us. Most especially we are not to listen to ourselves.

In all addictions there comes a time that is referred to as "hitting bottom." This is a time when the person collapses under the strain of the addiction. For a Messiah, hitting bottom often takes the form of burnout. As we go through a burnout experience, we receive a number of messages from a variety of sources, all urging us to abandon the addiction and turn to recovery. Most of us ignore these voices.

When in the Messiah Trap, I do not listen to anything except my compulsive drive to help others. I ignore the many messages my body sends me. Even though I may be having trouble sleeping, eating, and fighting off disease, I do not let my body rest. I ignore the warning messages my unconscious sends me through nightmares, daydreams, and impulsive desires. Instead of listening to what my feelings are trying to tell me, I become angry that I can't control my feelings. Depression and anxiety become a way of life.

Look over this list and see if you are experiencing these symptoms of burnout:

Messages from our bodies:

1. Physical exhaustion
2. Fatigue
3. Chronic colds or flus
4. Headaches
5. Rapid loss or gaining of weight
6. Sleeplessness or excessive sleepiness
7. Shortness of breath

Messages from our feelings:

1. Irritability and excessive anger
2. Anxiety; can extend to paranoia ("No one is helping; in fact, some of them are out to get me.")
3. Feeling omnipotent ("If they would only listen to me,

everything would be fine. I can see the problem, why can't they?")

4. Depression, sadness, loss of hope
5. Feeling abused, exploited, frustrated
6. Feeling isolated and unheard
7. Feeling indispensable, overly responsible, trapped
8. Boredom
9. Relationships feel like obligations rather than opportunities for intimacy

Messages from our behavior:

1. Verbally or physically attacking others
2. Impulsive, self-endangering behavior (for example, driving faster than usual)
3. Acting defensive or critical
4. Substance abuse (including the misuse of tranquilizers, sleeping pills, alcohol, and other drugs)
5. Shift in behavior (for example, becoming withdrawn when one is usually talkative)
6. Inability to enjoy anyone else's successes or joys
7. Entertaining fantasies of escape
8. Engaging in self-destructive relationships (for example, initiating an extramarital affair)
9. Becoming forgetful, easily confused, or irresponsible

Using this list, identify any burnout symptoms you may have. Assess to what degree you are experiencing these symptoms.

Carmen's burnout symptoms:

Messages from her body:

Sleeplessness
Loss of appetite
Chronic colds

Messages from her feelings:

Hopelessness
Feeling trapped

Messages from her behavior:

Irritable
Forgetful

My burnout symptoms:

Messages from my body:

Messages from my feelings:

Messages from my behavior:

Exercise 8:   **Learning to Solve Problems Effectively**

Instead of ignoring the messages we receive, those of us in recovery are learning to listen to and cooperate with these voices. Certainly not all the messages we receive are from God, and it is important to discern these messages carefully. However, most of us have been taught to distrust ourselves when, as creations of God, we are most wonderfully made.

It is important to listen to the messages you are receiving from yourself and from God. If you are exhibiting symptoms of burnout, it is critical that changes be made *now*, before more damage is done to your body, your spirit, and your relationships. What are the sources of stress in your life? Review your "tree" and see if there are branches that are in need of pruning. Is it time to let go of activities or relationships?

Take time to develop one thing you can do today that will help alleviate the stress in your life. Don't try to change your life overnight. Rather, take one step at a time. Ongoing problem solving is the most effective strategy for escaping Messiah Trap burnout.

The step Carmen will take today to alleviate some of the stress in her life:

I have felt overly stressed since I agreed to take on a special writing project. I will call those involved and arrange for more time to complete the project. If no more time is possible, I will resign from the project. As I let go of this responsibility, I will embrace the opportunity to have more time for renewal.

The step I will take today to alleviate some of the stress in my life:

Recovery Ritual

The process of letting go of the past and embracing renewal is complex and, at times, paradoxical. Only when the seed is planted and dies can it burst open and bring new life. Only when we give up can we receive new hope. Only when we cut back can we experience new growth.

Today's recovery ritual focuses on the paradoxical aspect of our recovery journey. Nature provides us with many examples of this process. I suggest that you draw a picture or create from magazine pictures a collage that depicts both winter (letting go) and spring (embracing renewal).

It may be helpful to divide a page in half, then draw or place pictures of winter on one side and draw or place pictures of spring on the other side. This ritual is just for you, so a perfect drawing is certainly not necessary; let your imagination play with the pictures or symbols you find in magazines; pick anything in nature that signals renewal to you. Feel free to create another ritual that honors both sides of this process. As we come to trust that renewal will follow, we will be better able to cooperate with, rather than control, the process of growth.

Carmen's recovery ritual:

I will make a collage of pictures depicting winter and spring. I will divide the page in half, with winter pictures on one side and spring pictures on the other. After I have pasted the pictures in place, I will write the word Trust *across the page as a bridge between the two. This will symbolize for me that it requires faith on my part to let go of the past and expect something better in the future.*

My recovery ritual:

Recovery Expression

Step 1:
Selecting Who to Tell About My Recovery Session

One of the major themes in this session has been opening ourselves up to a healthier type of intimacy. Since loving others is a critical part of any person's recovery, I have included an opportunity for deepening our relationships in every session. As with all the sessions, selecting those with whom we share is important.

Look over your previous sessions and see if a pattern is emerging. Do you usually choose the same person or do you select different people each time? In this session I recommend that you choose someone with whom you have not shared before. Since you are letting go of the past, which includes non-helpful relationships, this is a good time to reach out to someone new. Embrace a new future by opening the door to different and deeper relationships.

The person Carmen will talk to about her recovery session:

After my next support group meeting, I will invite one of the women I usually sit with out for coffee.

The person I will talk to about my recovery session:

Step 2:
Deciding What to Tell Others About My Recovery Session

Since you will be sharing with someone who is unfamiliar with your recovery journey, you may want to review the first session of this workbook. At the beginning, you developed an initial statement about what you intended to accomplish through this process. This may help you decide what to say to the person you have selected.

Be clear and concise in your description of your journey. Let the person know what it is you are requesting from him or her. You will need to be clear that you are asking for support, but not advice or approval. Communicate the value you place on the friendship. Welcome him or her as part of your support system.

What Carmen will tell about her recovery session:

I will say that I have wanted to spend time getting to know her better. I will show her my workbook and share briefly about a recent session.
I will explain that I am learning to let go of the past and open myself up to new relationships, which is one of the reasons I took the risk to invite her out to coffee. I value her support, though I am learning not to ask for advice or approval. I value her friendship and hope that we can share from time to time.

What I will tell about my recovery session:

Recovery Celebration

Many of the lessons we have learned in today's session have been taught to us through nature. The benefits of pruning come to us through an understanding of nature's way with trees, bushes, and other plant life. The need to let go and the promise of renewal are illustrated to us through the bleakness of winter and the celebration of spring.

Today's celebration may honor nature as one of our recovery instructors. You may want to go for a walk on the beach, in a garden, or through the woods. Take time to enjoy the fragrances—the flowers in the garden, the salt air of the ocean, or the pine scent of the forest. Listen to the birds sing, the waves crash, or the stream churn. If it is warm, you may want to go barefoot and feel the grass or sand beneath your feet. If it is cold, you may want to play in the snow. Celebrate nature with as many of your senses as possible—sight, sound, smell, touch—even taste if there is fruit to eat or water to drink.

Recovery Checklist

- ☐ I initiated the session with a recovery ritual
- ☐ I read pages 36–40 in *When Helping You Is Hurting Me*
- ☐ I identified difficulties I have in my peer and intimate relationships
- ☐ I further developed my ability to establish peer and intimate relationships
- ☐ I identified ways I am caught in the cycle of isolation
- ☐ I learned new ways to belong to a group while retaining a sense of self
- ☐ I assessed my drive for endless activity
- ☐ I learned new ways to take satisfaction in a job well done
- ☐ I identified how my addiction will lead me to burnout
- ☐ I developed a next step in solving problems more effectively
- ☐ I created a recovery ritual
- ☐ I selected who to tell about my recovery session
- ☐ I decided what to say about my recovery session
- ☐ I celebrated my progress

 Conclude the session with your recovery ritual.

Session 6

I Deserve Attention

Attending to My Inner Work

Initiate the session with your recovery ritual.

Our energy and attention are misdirected when we are caught in the Messiah Trap. This session will address one of the most serious ways we Messiahs misdirect our energy. Instead of attending to our interior journeys, we get sidetracked into exterior, compulsive caregiving. Instead of taking responsibility for ourselves, we become obsessed with managing the lives of others. Instead of cooperating with the interior guidance we receive, we feel compelled to control everyone in our lives.

Recovery Reading

The recommended reading: chapter 5, pages 41–55, in *When Helping You Is Hurting Me*.

Recovery Reflection

In the reading for today, seven kinds of Messiahs are described. Each of these Messiah styles misdirects our energy into the exterior in ways that are both hurtful to us and unhelpful to others:

I. The Pleaser

In any healthy relationship, it is important to be sensitive and nurturing. A Pleaser, however, takes this to an extreme and feels responsible for other people's happiness. When I am caught in the Pleaser trap, I feel that it is my job to make sure everyone else's life turns out right. If someone in the world is experiencing difficulty or unhappiness, I feel *guilty*. I don't even have to know that person. At times I can't watch the news because, if there is some disaster or tragedy, I feel as if I have failed to make the world a safe place.

As a Pleaser I secretly believe that other people are incompetent and unable to take responsibility for their own lives. Only I am capable of such responsibility. I take this responsibility very seriously and find myself consumed with everyone else's affairs. Instead of taking the time I need to cope with my own inner hurts and needs, my attention is riveted on the exterior—on everyone else's problems but my own.

2. The Rescuer

Not everyone who wears a beeper is a Rescuer. But there are a lot of us Rescuers wearing beepers because we want to be electronically connected to every emergency in our geographical area. We do not want to miss any crisis in which we could take charge and save the day.

Crises come into all our lives without warning. We all have emergencies that require dropping everything and shifting our priorities. But if you have four or five crises before lunch, I suspect you might be someone who is addicted to rescuing. We Rescuers get a wonderful adrenaline rush from our dashing around. In fact, I believe this is one of the most difficult Messiah styles to overcome because the physical high we get from dealing with a crisis can be strongly addictive.

We Rescuers love to be out on freeways changing tires, dashing to airports, delivering last-minute packages, leaping from bed in the middle of the night to stop a suicide attempt—anything but sitting quietly and attending to our own inner pain.

3. The Giver

Givers feel responsible for meeting the material needs of those around them. We Givers feel compelled to give anything we have to someone who may be in need. If you are a Giver, the only reason you have any material possessions is because no one has asked you for them yet! As soon as someone asks, we Givers give.

If we do keep anything for ourselves, our guilt can be tremendous. Living under the threat of being considered "selfish," we focus our attention on meeting the material needs of others. We are usually busy delivering hot meals to shut-ins, going door to door to collect funds for world hunger, or taking the bus (because we loaned our car to a needy friend). We have nothing left over for ourselves.

4. The Counselor

This is a style I developed into an art form. I know how to turn any social situation into a counseling session. I don't flippantly ask, "So how are ya' doin'?" I look the person deep in the eyes and ask, "So tell me, *how are you doing*?" A response of "fine" does not interest me. I want to hear about the divorce, the last suicide attempt, the depression, and the pain. As a Counselor, I love to hear about your problems because it gives me an excuse to avoid facing my own.

5. The Protector

We Protectors spend our time protecting other people—usually from the truth. Since we consider ourselves to be stronger than anyone else, we believe that only we are able to know what is really going on. If we believe some situation is too painful, we will withhold information. But if we think something we have heard may be helpful, we Protectors will violate confidentiality and pass on the word. It is easy for a Protector to become embroiled in gossip and information networks but not take the time to listen to his or her own interior messages.

6. The Teacher

A Teacher is someone who goes from group to group, meeting to meeting, session to session, and yet never experiences genuine intimacy. We are busy outlining agendas, organizing our teams, collecting our evaluation sheets, and giving speeches. You will rarely, however, find Messiah Teachers paying attention to the lessons to be learned in their own inner lives.

7. The Crusader

I believe that one aspect of a balanced life is contribution to the larger community. However, we Crusaders place a "cause" at the center of our lives, throwing ourselves grossly out of balance. Our cause is usually something positive. But even positive commitments can be made into addictions. Soon everything we do, say, and feel is determined by our cause—whether that cause be campaigning for a new law, advocating for helpless children, or trying to get a spouse to stop drinking. We Crusaders have no time for quiet reflection or attending to our inner work.

Exercise 1:

Identifying Our Primary Messiah Styles

At one time or another, I have adopted all seven of the Messiah styles. Review the list and select one style with which you seem to identify most strongly. It may be that you relate to more than one, but please select just one to work through the following exercises. You can always return and repeat the process with another style.

Select your style. Describe how engaging in this kind of helping behavior keeps you from attending to your own interior growth.

Carmen's style:

Counselor

How Carmen's style helps her avoid her inner work:

By playing the Counselor I can spend my time struggling with other people's problems and thereby avoid looking at my own or even paying attention to my inner pain. When I feel sorry for other people it helps me hide my own inner sorrow.

My style:

How my style helps me avoid my inner work:

Exercise 2:   *Creating a Portrait of Our Messiah Styles*

Sit quietly for a moment with your eyes closed. Imagine how you look when you are performing your Messiah role. In the following space, create a self-portrait. You may want to use colored pens or pencils and draw a picture of your Messiah style. Or you may choose to make a collage by cutting out pictures from magazines. Use your imagination!

A portrait of Carmen's Messiah style:

Carmen the "Counselor" listening . . .

A portrait of my Messiah style:

Escaping the Messiah Trap

Exercise 3:   ***Talking with Your Inner Messiah***

In this exercise we are going to use a technique called active imagination. I often use interior dialogue to better understand myself. This is a very powerful technique because we can gain access to unconscious material that may ordinarily elude us. Before you proceed with this exercise I would like to emphasize how powerful I believe this technique to be. You may receive information about past experiences or connect to strong feelings. I do not recommend that you use this technique without the support of a therapist or group. If you are not in therapy or attending a support group, it would be better to skip this exercise. With others to assist you in sorting out the facts and dealing with feelings, this technique can bring substantial healing into your life.

Take a look at the portrait you have created. Imagine this is a person with whom you can talk. There are a variety of ways to talk with your inner Messiah. Sometimes I use my computer so that I can keep a record of the conversation. At other times, I write the dialogue out in longhand. Some people I know record the conversation on a tape recorder. Sometimes I merely "think" through the conversation, but I have found that keeping a record of some kind is the most helpful. (For more comprehensive instruction on the use of active imagination you may want to read Robert A. Johnson's *Inner Work: Using Dreams and Active Imagination for Personal Growth*.)

Decide which approach you will take. The following questions may help you begin your conversation: Do you have a special name? How are you feeling today? How do you help me? What is it that you need from me?

Carmen's conversation with her inner Messiah:

Carmen: Hello, Counselor. I would like to talk to you. Will you talk with me?

Counselor: I have been waiting to talk with you for a very long time. You are always so busy with everyone else, you never listen to me.

Carmen: I didn't realize that you wanted to talk. I am listening now.

Counselor: There is much I want to tell you, and I hope we can continue to talk. So many other people catch your attention, you don't notice that you also need help.

Carmen: But I don't really need that much help. I'm the person everyone else comes to for advice.

Counselor: Yes, Carmen, we do have problems and I want you to trust me enough to listen to what I have to say. I am the part of you that can comfort you and help you face the very hard issues ahead.

Carmen: What you say scares me some. I am afraid to look at my problems too closely. Somehow I don't feel like I deserve your attention, or anyone's for that matter. What if I don't know what to do?

Counselor: I can help you if you'll let me. Then we can face your shame about not deserving attention and your guilt about not being able to help everyone.

Carmen: Okay, I promise to talk with you again. And if you will help me face these issues, then I will try to trust you.

My conversation with my inner Messiah:

Recovery Ritual

Review the conversation you have had with your inner Messiah. Select some aspect that is especially meaningful to you. Create a ritual that symbolizes the insight, encouragement, or other gift you may have received from your inner Messiah.

Carmen's recovery ritual:

I will draw a picture of my inner Counselor holding me on her lap. Around the picture I will write words I associate with her: comfort, safety, wisdom, guidance, answers, courage, acceptance, forgiveness, confession, assistance, hope. I will post this picture on my bathroom mirror to remind me that I have inner resources to help me face my problems.

My recovery ritual:

Recovery Expression

Step 1:
Selecting Who to Tell About My Recovery Session

I have found that my experience with active imagination is quite personal and meaningful. It is important to select a person who understands the power and validity of this inner-work technique. You may want to ask your inner Messiah to recommend a person with whom you can share today's session. You may decide to take your workbook to therapy and share this session with your therapist. This is especially helpful if this exercise has triggered any strong, confusing, and difficult feelings. I have also found it helpful to share what I have learned through active imagination with my support group or with a few, close friends.

The person Carmen will talk to about her recovery session:

My support group

The person I will talk to about my recovery session:

Step 2:
Deciding What to Tell Others About My Recovery Session

When you talk with some people, you may decide to summarize what you learned in today's session. With others, you may choose to read the conversation. Be very selective about who you allow to read any conversation you have with an inner character. Please do not feel obligated to share these conversations with anyone, as they are private and personal. Share only what makes you feel comfortable. The purpose of sharing is to obtain the support you need and deserve, not to invade your privacy.

What Carmen will tell about her recovery session:

I will not read my conversation to my support group. I will, however, summarize what I have learned. I will tell my support group that I am realizing it is time to face my own problems more directly. Admitting I have problems frightens me. At the same time, my inner Counselor has reminded me that I am a competent and resourceful person. Many people have turned to me for support because I am accepting and helpful. I am able to use those same skills on my own behalf. So while I am a little frightened by the thought of facing my problems, I am also encouraged by the realization that I have many interior resources to call upon throughout this process.

What I will tell about my recovery session:

Recovery Celebration

This transition to the inner life is often very demanding. But once you have begun to understand and participate in your own inner journey, you will experience a new appreciation for the strengths and resources that you have within. You are now entering into a new world and you can celebrate by taking yourself to an adventurous or fantasylike place. Maybe this could mean visiting a zoo, going to an animated or adventure movie, enjoying a theme park, or exploring some new part of nature.

Recovery Checklist

- ☐ I initiated the session with a recovery ritual
- ☐ I read pages 41–55 in *When Helping You Is Hurting Me*
- ☐ I identified my primary Messiah style
- ☐ I created a portrait of my inner Messiah
- ☐ I had a conversation with my inner Messiah
- ☐ I created a recovery ritual
- ☐ I selected who to tell about my recovery session
- ☐ I decided what to say about my recovery session
- ☐ I celebrated my progress

 Conclude the session with your recovery ritual.

Session 7

I Deserve Safety

Listening to My Hurting Inner Child

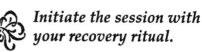

I admit that, for years, I avoided my inner work because I was afraid of the silence. Whenever I slowed down and allowed the noise in my life to decrease, I would hear in the back of my mind the sound of a small child crying. Instead of being drawn to those cries, I ran from them, afraid I would drown in the tears. So I turned up the volume in my life, in a hectic pace of compulsive caregiving. I was willing to listen to other people cry over their pain. Any voice was welcome, no matter how sad, except for one. I would not tolerate the sound of my own voice crying.

Recovery Reading

The recommended reading: chapters 2 and 3, pages 8–28, in *When Helping You Is Hurting Me.*

Recovery Reflection

I have discovered that there are two ways to fall into the Messiah Trap. You could have had a "happy" childhood or a traumatic childhood. A "happy" childhood is one in which no major trauma or problem can be identified. In fact, a "happy" childhood is one in which we had no childhood at all. We were so busy acting like little adults, trying to please our parents, teachers, baby-sitters, and relatives, that we never had the chance to be who we actually were—little kids trying to grow up. Putting a child into an adult role prematurely is equivalent to destroying that child's childhood. The day you and I were treated as adults, our childhoods came to an end and we were set up for the Messiah Trap.

Those raised in overtly troubled families also are set up for the Trap. Children who have been traumatized realize that there is no adult to rely on for protection or nurturance. In this society we usually blame the victim for the abuse. A victim of physical abuse may hear, "If you hadn't spilled your milk, I wouldn't have slapped you across the face" or "If you had cleaned your room like I told you, I wouldn't have jammed your head against the wall." Children of alcoholic parents may hear, "Why did you bother your mother with your problems? If you upset her, she'll start drinking again!" Young children who have been sexually abused have been accused of being too provocative or seductive with "Why didn't you resist your father, you little tramp?"

Some children who have been traumatized respond by becoming abusive and violent themselves. But others, like many who have fallen into the Messiah Trap, take a different route. We believe that we really are to blame for the trauma and that, if we had been "good," we would not have been hurt. In an effort to protect ourselves, we try to be perfect, pleasing every adult in our lives. We fall into the Trap when we tell ourselves unconsciously, "If I can be good enough, I will be safe." This is a variation on the first Messiah lie, "If I don't do it, it won't get done."

Of course, no one can be good enough to be safe. "Safety" and "goodness" are not connected, although many of us pretend they are and defend such an idea through various religious and philosophical dogmas. Abusive behavior is the sole responsibility of the abuser. Only when abusive people take responsibility for and put an end to their assaults will the world be a safe place in which to live. Rather than trying to please someone who is abusive, we can better protect ourselves by attending to the warning signals and listening to our own feelings. While self-protection skills can be learned, "goodness" is not an adequate defense against a powerful and cruel assailant.

Since we cannot protect ourselves by being "good," we are vulnerable to being re-victimized. Consequently, our self-esteem is further eroded. We further doubt our importance in the world, feeling unloved and insignificant. The second side of the Messiah Trap is communicated to us: "Everyone else's needs take priority over mine."

Whether we were taught the lies of the Messiah Trap through violent or nonviolent means, the result is the same—we become addicted to a self-destructive way of life that gives us no time to attend to our own needs. The child within us, the one who was robbed of the opportunity to delight in the joys of growing up in a loving and safe home, is still trapped in the sadness, in the terror, in the pain.

Exercise 1:   *Identifying Our Inner Child*

A variety of family systems can set children up for the Messiah Trap. It is possible that you experienced more than one of these situations when you were a child. For today's session, I would like you to select one experience or situation you recall as a child, rather than try to deal with your childhood in any comprehensive way. In fact, if this is your first time doing inner-work exercises that relate to your inner child, I recommend that you select a memory that seems mild or minimally traumatic. I do not suggest that you tackle a difficult memory until you are familiar with and skilled at interacting with your inner child.

As with the previous session, I again urge you to approach your interior world with respect and caution. It is especially important that your inner child be provided with the safety and adult supervision needed, the kind of care you most likely did not receive when you were a child. I recommend that, if you have yet to secure a therapist and a support group, you discontinue working these exercises and spend the session developing a proper support system. If you have a therapist and support group, I believe it will be most helpful for you to ask for special support during this time.

The exercises in this session can be used again and again to help you work through other troubling childhood memories. It is important to go slowly, giving yourself all the time and support you need. Remember, you are entering into a child's world, with a child's view of time. Children live life at a different pace than adults. As you learn to love your inner child, you will learn to move more slowly, more playfully, and with more awareness of the flowers.

Describe a childhood experience in which (1) you were put into an adult role prematurely and/or (2) you were abused and then blamed for the abuse.

Carmen's experience:

When I was fourteen I attended a summer camp with my friends. On the first day, our counselor became ill and had to go home. The camp director pulled me aside and asked me to act as the counselor for my cabin. I was proud of being asked and readily said yes. As I look back on it now, I realize that this changed my relationships with my friends. They no longer treated me as one of them. Since my friends had ostracized me, I tried to hang out with the other counselors, who were all much older than I. They tried to be nice to me, but I could tell they didn't really want me around. I spent the week feeling lonely, as an outsider looking in while everyone else had a good time. This is an example of being placed in an adult caregiving role prematurely.

My experience:

Exercise 2:   *Creating a Portrait of My Inner Child*

In this exercise, concentrate on the same childhood experience. As we recall one childhood memory, other experiences often come to mind.

Since we may have had experiences throughout our childhoods that set us up for the Messiah Trap, we may find that our inner child appears to us sometimes as being one age and, at other times, as being a different age. You may want to jot a note to yourself so that you don't forget these various experiences. In order not to become overwhelmed or confused by various experiences, however, I caution you to focus solely on one experience in your childhood. Allow the child you have identified in the previous exercise ample time to communicate with you.

Sit quietly for a moment with your eyes closed and remember how you looked during the experience previously described. How old were you? How did you wear your hair? What clothes were you wearing? In the following space, create a self-portrait. You may want to use colored pens or pencils or paste a collage from magazine pictures.

A portrait of Carmen when she was fourteen at summer camp:

A portrait of myself as a child:

Escaping the Messiah Trap

Exercise 3:   ***Talking with Your Inner Child***

This exercise will use the technique of active imagination. In the previous session, I suggested several approaches, such as using a computer or writing out the conversation in longhand. I have found that one way my inner child communicates with me is through the use of my nondominant hand; that is, I use my left hand since I am normally right-handed. Writing with the non-dominant hand can access our childlike self. I have special paper that I use for these conversations, paper that has large colorful lines. I also have purchased a set of colored pencils especially for my inner child. I write to her in my dominant hand and use my nondominant hand to write out what she says to me. This takes more time than other approaches because I cannot write as fast with my nondominant hand. I have found, however, that taking this time helps me to focus on myself as the child I once was and to identify my special needs. If you choose not to use this approach, the computer or longhand is also workable.

Once you start talking with your inner child, the conversation will take on a direction of its own. If your inner child feels safe and acknowledged, he or she may tell you quite a bit about events, feelings, and needs. To get started, you may want to use the following questions: Do you have a special name? What grade are you in? What do you like to do? How are you feeling today? What do you need from me?

Carmen's conversation with her inner child:

Hello. Do you have a special name?
My name is Carmencita.
What do you like to do, Carmencita?
I don't get to play very often because I help out a lot.
What kinds of things do you do when you help out?
I help the grown ups take care of the other kids. I have to be extra good so the grown ups will trust me.
Is it important for the grownups to trust you?
Oh yes! If I disappoint them I'd feel awful.
How are you feeling today?
Oh, a little sad and lonely. I don't really have anyone to hang out with. My friends say I act like a big shot now that I'm a counselor. The other counselors are lots older than I am so I'm pretty much on my own.
What do you need from me right now?
Would you hang out with me? I need a friend.

My conversation with my inner child:

Escaping the Messiah Trap

Recovery Ritual

Review the conversation you have had with your inner child. If there is something special that stands out, you may want to create a ritual to honor that aspect. If you promised to help your inner child in any way, it may be helpful to use a ritual to reinforce your promise. Or you may choose to honor your inner child by creating a ritual that shows your caring and appreciation of what she or he has endured.

Carmen's recovery ritual:

I will get a picture of myself when I was at summer camp. I will frame the picture and put it on my nightstand. When I see this picture I will let it remind me of my inner child and that there is healing for me to do. This will help me remember to use active imagination with her in the future and to attend to her needs more consistently.

My recovery ritual:

Recovery Expression

Step 1:
Selecting Who to Tell About My Recovery Session

As I have mentioned before, it is very important to have additional support when dealing with childhood memories. Many people, especially those in the recovery movement, are familiar with the concept of inner child. When thinking over with whom to share this part of your journey, be careful to select someone who can appreciate and support inner-child work. It will not be helpful to share with someone who does not understand or support this approach. I recommend that, in addition to any friends or family you select, you share this experience with your therapist.

The person Carmen will talk to about her recovery session:

My close friend and my therapist

The person I will talk to about my recovery session:

Step 2:
Deciding What to Tell Others About My Recovery Session

Deciding what to share is an important step. You are not in any way obligated to let other people read your inner conversations. Feel free to summarize what you have learned. However, if you feel comfortable, you may show the writing to a person you trust.

What Carmen will tell about her recovery session:

I will not show my writing to my friend, but I will show it to my therapist. I will tell them both that I learned more about why I feel so lonely when I am with a group of peers. Even though it felt good at first to be singled out as a teenager as special and responsible, I soon felt different and unacceptable. No one wanted me once I was placed in this adult role. I did not experience being a part of the fun. Instead, I felt too old for the teenagers my age and too young for the other counselors.

What I will tell about my recovery session:

Recovery Celebration

Now that you have made contact with your inner child, it may be easier for you to come up with fun ideas for this part of the session. Ask your inner child what he or she would like to do. Maybe drawing a picture would be fun, or watching cartoons. Perhaps a run in the park to fly kites. Your inner child may want to make mud pies or dance to loud music. Embrace your inner child and have a great time!

Recovery Checklist

- ☐ I initiated the session with a recovery ritual
- ☐ I read pages 8–28 in *When Helping You Is Hurting Me*
- ☐ I identified my inner child
- ☐ I created a portrait of my inner child
- ☐ I had a conversation with my inner child
- ☐ I created a recovery ritual
- ☐ I selected who to tell about my recovery session
- ☐ I decided what to say about my recovery session
- ☐ I celebrated my progress

Conclude the session with your recovery ritual.

Session 8

I Say Yes to Myself

Identifying My Own Needs and Wants

Even though we Messiahs are usually talented and competent people, we have dedicated ourselves to developing skills that focus on meeting other people's needs, not our own. Since we have tried to earn our worth by pleasing other people, we have developed the skills needed to glean what other people need and want. When asked to meet our own needs, or even to identify what we may want, we Messiahs often come up with a total blank. I once asked a friend of mine, "Tell me, what is it that you want?" She very wisely responded, "To be honest with you, I want whatever you want me to want."

Many of us have never been asked the question I asked my friend. As children, we were not allowed to express our own needs. And we were certainly not encouraged to put effort into meeting our needs, if, by chance, we had known what they were. As adults, we are as inexperienced and unskilled as young children when it comes to addressing our needs and wants.

Recovery Reading

The recommended reading: reread chapter 5, pages 41–55, in *When Helping You Is Hurting Me.*

Recovery Reflection

I recommended rereading chapter 5 so that the Messiah styles will be fresh in your mind. Each of these styles gives to others what we need to have for ourselves.

I. The Pleaser

Pleasers are people who, underneath the surface, feel neglected and overlooked. When we become obsessed with making other people happy, it is a signal to us that we are actually distressed and displeased with our own lives. If you consider yourself a Messiah Pleaser, it may be helpful for you to put more energy into pleasing yourself. We Pleasers need to find out what makes us happy and put energy into bringing good experiences into our lives.

2. The Rescuer

We Rescuers are busy trying to make the world a safe place for people in crisis. Our attempts to bring order to the chaos are a clue that, inside us, we feel threatened and fearful. Unable to tolerate danger, Rescuers usually harbor a secret desire for more safety for themselves. If you find yourself rescuing those around you, I suggest that more of your effort be put into identifying your own fears. We Rescuers are in need of protection and safety, a need that is overlooked in our obsession with the safety of others.

3. The Giver

Givers are generous people who are acutely aware of other people's material needs. Often we Givers feel guilty about the material possessions we have, feeling that we do not deserve what we have. If you see yourself as a Messiah Giver, it is likely that you need to be affirmed in tangible ways, such as giving yourself flowers or buying that shirt you've been wanting. We are all equally important and valuable. It may be time to shed the guilt and to learn how to enjoy the good and pleasurable in this world.

4. The Counselor

We Counselors listen to other people, helping them sort through confusing problems and feelings. As children, many Counselors were expected to listen to their parents and siblings talk about their problems, yet were not given a turn to talk. If you are a Counselor, it is very likely that you need someone to listen to you. You may need to experience the same acceptance and nurturance you have so readily given to others.

5. The Protector

We Protectors are aware that words can hurt and so we try to protect others from harm. Often Protectors are those who, as children, were given too much information too soon. If you are a Protector, you may need help sorting out the truth for yourself. You may need to ask someone to help you, someone who can provide safety and protection.

6. The Teacher

Like Protectors, we Teachers are concerned with the truth. We feel compelled to understand how the world works and then spread the word as widely as possible. If you are a Teacher, you may feel that no one is available to help you sort out the facts from the fiction. It may be time to become the student and allow yourself the opportunity to learn and grow.

7. The Crusader

We Crusaders are dedicated and passionate people. Fierce in our abhorrence of injustice, we fight for what we believe. If you are a Crusader, it may be time to take up a new cause—yourself. Combating the injustice and abuse you have endured is a most worthy cause, one to which I encourage you to dedicate yourself.

Exercise I: ***Asking My Inner Messiah What I Need***

In session 6, "Attending to My Inner Work," you had a conversation with your inner Messiah. I would like you to invite your inner Messiah back for another discussion. Please review that session, paying attention to the drawing you made. After you visualize your inner Messiah, engage in an active imagination session. I would like you to ask your inner Messiah these questions:

1. What do you give to other people?
2. What do you believe I need for myself?
3. What do you need from me?

Carmen's conversation with her inner Messiah:

Carmen: Hello, Counselor. I would like to talk with you again. Will you talk with me?

Counselor: Yes, I am very glad to hear from you again.

Carmen: I'd like to ask you some questions. What is it that you give to other people?

Counselor: I give them a safe place to talk and wise counsel.

Carmen: What do you believe I need for myself?

Counselor: I believe you need what I give to other people. You also need a safe place to share and sort through alternatives.

Carmen: And how about you? What is it that you need from me?

Counselor: Believe it or not, I need what you need. I would very much like to talk with you more. It would do us both so much good if we spent more time caring for each other rather than pretending we have no needs.

Carmen: I agree. I'll be back and we can talk again.

My conversation with my inner Messiah:

Exercise 2:   ***Asking My Inner Child What I Need***

Messiahs often have trouble identifying our own needs and
wants. Active imagination is an excellent technique for reveal-
ing unconscious or unidentified issues. In the same manner as
above, I would like you to have a conversation with your inner
child. Ask your inner child the following three questions:

1. What do you need from me?
2. What kind of things do you like to do?
3. What do you wish you could give to me?

Carmen's conversation with her inner child:

Carmen: Hello, how have you been since last we spoke?
Inner Child: Okay, I guess. No one pays much attention to
me.

Carmen: What do you need from me?
Inner Child: I wish you would spend more time with me.
I've got lots of questions about growing up but no one takes the
time to explain things to me. I also wish you were around more
to do fun things with me.

Carmen: What kind of things would you like to do?

Inner Child: I like listening to music and reading magazines. There are some good videos out now I'd like to see.

Carmen: I think spending time with you could be a lot of fun.

Inner Child: Do you really think so? Most people don't. Even some of the kids my age think I am too grown up or something. I'd like to spend time with friends my own age. I've noticed you don't spend much time with friends either.

Carmen: I think you are really smart. If you could give me a gift, what would it be?

Inner Child: I think I'd give you a vacation with some fun-loving friends so you could dance and laugh and watch the sunset.

Carmen: That is a wonderful gift. But I would only take it if you would come along and join in the fun.

My conversation with my inner child:

Escaping the Messiah Trap

Exercise 3: ***Identifying What I Want and Need***

In the previous two exercises, you have given your inner Messiah and inner child an opportunity to identify some of your needs and wants. Review these conversations and list clearly what you learned about yourself in these exercises.

What Carmen needs and wants:

1. Someone to listen to me
2. Wise counsel
3. Time spent with myself
4. Playtime with my friends
5. A vacation

What I need and want:

I have identified my own need for play and enjoyment of friends. It is possible that your inner Messiah and child have helped you identify needs that are more serious and more difficult to handle. These may include the need to end a significant relationship, the need to change jobs, the need to confront someone who has hurt you, or the need for more intimacy. Feel free to use these techniques to identify a variety of needs and desires that may include the serious as well as the more playful.

Exercise 4:   ***Learning to Say No to Obligation***

It is not uncommon for someone to come up to me after a presentation and say, "I really identify with what you have said and I know I should take better care of myself, but I just don't have the time. How can I take on even more responsibility?"

It is true that many of us Messiahs are so overextended that we have neither the time nor the energy to have fun. The thought of doing something nice for ourselves feels more like another obligation than an opportunity. Before we can experience the birth of a new way of life, we must first face the death of the old. Again, it is time to cooperate with the process of growth with its death and resurrection cycle.

Learning to say no can be a kind of death to us Messiahs. We need to "prune" back our activities and obligations so that a place is cleared for new, more nurturing experiences. Saying no can be very difficult and guilt producing.

Think back on a conversation you had recently in which you said yes to a request when you really wanted to say no. Write out, word for word, what the other person said to you when he or she asked you for help. Stop there. Do not write what you said in response.

What the person said when he or she asked Carmen for help:

Someone from my church called and asked if I would volunteer some time with the youth group on a night I had planned to spend reading and relaxing. She said, "Carmen, we really need someone with your experience with teenagers. You know how much these kids need positive role models. Couldn't you help us out just this once?"

What the person said when he or she asked me for help:

Next, I would like you to write down how you felt while you were listening to this request.

Carmen's feelings:

On one hand I felt complimented that she saw me as a good role model. But on the other hand I felt trapped, obligated, and guilty for wanting to spend time on myself. She told me that these kids needed me and I felt like I was being selfish. But I really did not want to get involved in the youth program. I knew she was asking me to volunteer for one night only, but I suspected that she would be calling again and again. I wanted more time for my own recovery.

My feelings:

We Messiahs often struggle with conflicting feelings. If you are like me, you feel both a push and a pull. One technique I use, when I am not sure whether I want to participate or not, is to say, "Let me look at my schedule and I'll call you in a day or two." This gives me a couple of days to sort through how I really feel about taking on a new task. If I find that I want to participate, I can call and agree. But if I decide I would rather not, I have a couple of days to figure out how I will say no.

Since I asked you to select a situation in which you said yes when you really wanted to say no, I am assuming that you felt more negative than positive feelings about agreeing to this request. In the next section, I would like you to write out how you could have said no.

How Carmen can say no:

Thank you for asking me. It is quite a compliment to be considered for this job. However, I have already made a commitment for that evening. I need to decline.

How I can say no:

Exercise 5:   **Learning to Say Yes to Myself**

Oddly enough, saying yes can be as difficult as saying no. We feel so compelled to say yes to others and no to ourselves that many of us feel guilt-ridden if we reverse this process. It is important for us to learn how to say yes to ourselves.

Since it may be difficult, at first, to address our own needs and wants, I have used a technique that may help you. If I imagine that I am actually saying yes to someone else, it is easier for me to take time for myself. In the previous exercises, both our inner Messiahs and our inner children told us what they needed from us. Select one of your inner characters and tell him or her that you intend to help meet his or her needs.

Carmen's inner conversation:

Carmen: You told me that you enjoy spending time with your friends and listening to music.

Inner Child: Yes, I need some time to relax and play.

Carmen: I think that you deserve to have fun with your friends. I want to help you get that need met.

Inner Child: That is great! How can we do that?

Carmen: Let's call some of our friends and see who is free to go out on Friday night.

Inner Child: Don't you plan to work that night?

Carmen: I had planned to but I have changed my mind. Instead, I am going to take us both out for a fun evening.

My inner conversation:

Recovery Ritual

Develop a ritual that will serve as a reminder of your promise to address your identified need. For example, you may want to write your promise on a 3 x 5 card and post it on your mirror. Be sure to keep your word to yourself, to your inner Messiah, and to your inner child. Use this ritual as a reminder that, once you are committed to addressing your own needs and wants, it is important to follow through.

Recovery Expression

Step 1:
Selecting Who to Tell About My Personal Recovery Session

Coming to the place where we can identify our own needs and wants is a crucial step in the recovery process. I have been surprised at the reactions I have received from people in my life, once I began to express what I have needed and wanted. Some people welcome honest and straightforward communication. But I do need to warn you that others will find our newfound skill to be offensive or upsetting.

Saying no to other people in order to make way for your own needs may also result in negative reactions. To deal effectively with possible criticism, you may need extra support through this time. I recommend that you share this session with those you can count on for support and understanding.

Not all reactions will be negative, of course. Some people will be ready to enjoy the changes. If, as I did in this exercise, you identified needs that are best met through interacting with other people, it might be appropriate to include them in the fun!

Step 2:
Deciding What to Tell Others About My Recovery Session

Deciding what to share about this session is a matter of personal discretion. If you identified a more serious need, an intimate discussion may be best. On the other hand, you may have discovered that you need to have more fun. Instead of having a serious talk with a friend, it may be time to simply ask that person to go out for an enjoyable evening.

What Carmen will tell about her recovery session:

I will call a couple of my friends and simply say that I learned in my session that I have a need to enjoy myself this Friday night. I will then talk about what we might do together for a fun time.

What I will tell about my recovery session:

Recovery Celebration

The skills covered in this session may be the most important for us Messiahs. The core of our problem lies in our inability to identify and care for ourselves in legitimate and helpful ways. The steps we took today are significant and worthy of a grand celebration! I urge you to take time with this part of the session and develop an experience that truly honors what you have accomplished today.

Recovery Checklist

☐ I initiated the session with a recovery ritual
☐ I reread chapter 5 in *When Helping You Is Hurting Me*
☐ I asked my inner Messiah what I need
☐ I asked my inner child what I need
☐ I identified what I want and need
☐ I learned to say no to obligation
☐ I learned to say yes to myself
☐ I created a recovery ritual
☐ I selected who to tell about my recovery session
☐ I decided what to say about my recovery session
☐ I celebrated my progress

 Conclude the session with your recovery ritual.

Initiate the session with your recovery ritual.

We Messiahs are fundamentally caring people. Few of us can tolerate seeing someone else in pain. When someone is being hurt, I am quickly moved to action, having no difficulty confronting someone I consider dangerous or harmful.

As I have moved through my own recovery, however, I have been confronted with my own abusive and neglectful actions. My recovery journey was originally motivated by the overwhelming pain I experienced. However, as I began to see how my addiction so deeply damaged those I was trying to help, my resolve to face my addiction grew even stronger. I now use my legitimate caring for others as further motivation to escape the Messiah Trap.

I must warn you right now that this session promises to be a difficult, even painful one. But this session can also bring profound healing and new opportunities for honest and satisfying intimacy. I believe we can be positive and healing forces in this world—but only once we are free from the self-deception that our codependency is in any way helpful, positive, or benign.

Recovery Reading

The recommended reading: chapter 6, pages 56–72, in *When Helping You Is Hurting Me* and the Twelve Steps in Appendix A of this workbook.

Recovery Reflection

Several years ago a friend of mine gathered up his courage and confronted me about hurting him. "When you try to help me," he explained with a hurt yet angry edge to his voice, "you make me feel so stupid. You tell me what I should do to resolve a situation, and I'll admit that most of the time your insight is accurate. It's not what you say as much as how you say it to me. I feel so dim-witted for not seeing the solution myself. I come away feeling like a failure and thoroughly dependent upon you! I ask myself, What would I do without Carmen? I'd be left on my own and I'm clearly not capable of dealing with my life alone."

I listened politely but secretly discounted everything he said. I didn't have much faith in his insight. Although I would not have said it out loud, I doubted very seriously that he actually could get by without me. To give him the benefit of the doubt, however, I agreed to ask several more of my friends about this issue. I had every confidence that no one else would view my efforts to help as being hurtful. To give this experiment an ample chance, I contacted seven of my closest friends.

Only a few days had passed before I came back, sad and somber, to acknowledge that my confrontative friend was indeed accurate in his assessment. I had asked my seven friends, "Have you found that my helping you has undermined your self-esteem? Do you come away feeling inadequate? Would you consider me arrogant?" All seven answered with a resounding "*Yes!*"

Some of my friends were gentle with me while others took the opportunity to unload years of anger and resentment toward me and my arrogant way of helping. In shock, I listened to story after story, reaching back into my youth, in which I had damaged those I wanted to help. I came to see that the gifts I offered had not been freely given. I secretly expected to be honored as the wisest, most competent, and most important person in my friends' lives. My friends were left feeling fearful, inadequate, and excessively dependent.

Even though years have passed since I was first confronted with my damaging behavior, I must keep a consistent watch over my so-called helping activities. When I fall prey to the first lie of the Messiah Trap (If I don't do it, it won't get done), it is impossible for me to view other people as competent. After all, I am the only one who can do it, even if "it" turns out to be taking responsibility for someone else's life. Unconsciously, I believe that everyone would live a better life if I were in charge. The world would be a safer place if only I were given control.

The help I offer is laced with this self-deception. An inflated sense of my power and importance is communicated to everyone who comes into my life. My arrogance erodes other people's self-esteem, as I unintentionally let them know that only I can run their lives properly.

The second Messiah lie (Everyone else's needs take priority over mine) motivates me even further to undermine the self-esteem of those I am "helping." Alongside my arrogance is a terrifying sense of inadequacy. Fear of abandonment haunts me, and so I try to bind others to me by intensifying their feelings of neediness. Although I say I want others to heal and grow, I am secretly fearful that those in my life will outgrow me and leave me behind. If my loved ones realize they are not dependent upon me for survival, so the lie goes, then what guarantee do I have that they will stay?

Out of my lack of self-esteem, I unconsciously wound and cripple the self-esteem of others. Because I feel unlovable, I destroy any opportunity to receive love, freely given. Although I actually want them to love me, I settle instead for having them need me. When caught in the Messiah Trap, I am unable to see that my need to be needed is hurtful to others.

You may hurt people in a different way than I do. But I have no doubt that, if you have fallen into the Messiah Trap, you hurt others every time you try to help. No one may be telling you that you are hurtful. Or maybe people have tried to let you know, but you ignored or minimized their comments the way I tried to disregard my friend's confrontation.

Exercise 1:   *Identifying Ways My Messiah Style Hurts Others*

In session 6, you identified your primary Messiah style. As acknowledged, most of us engage in more than one of these addictive styles. You may want to work through the following exercises with other Messiah styles at another time. For this session, however, I urge you to select the Messiah style that you worked with previously so that a depth of understanding can develop.

Please select your Messiah style.

Carmen's Messiah style:

Counselor

My Messiah style:

If needed, review the section in chapter 6 of *When Helping You Is Hurting Me* that pertains directly to your style. Ponder this information carefully and identify the various ways your style may hurt other people.

How Carmen's Messiah style can hurt others:

One way the Counselor can hurt others is by promoting one-sided intimacy. This may not seem like a major problem, but, in fact, a Counselor robs others of the most important aspect of life—an opportunity to know and love one another. When I hide behind the Counselor mask, no one has the chance to accurately see or experience the real person. Genuine love is impossible. Everyone loses when a Counselor is in control.

A second way Counselors hurt others is by ignoring those without problems to solve. Since Counselors feel worthwhile and needed only when they are counseling, they become uncomfortable in conversations that are not problem-solving in orientation. "Small talk" or conversations that may result in spontaneous intimacy are avoided. Counselors leave those who are capable of balanced intimacy to look for someone with a problem to solve.

A third way Counselors hurt others is by undermining others' self-esteem. To feel needed, Counselors try to make themselves indispensable to the lives of others. This cripples the development and growth of those who come to the Counselor for assistance. Without realizing it, the Counselor drags other people into the snare of the Messiah Trap.

How my Messiah style can hurt others:

Exercise 2:   *Identifying Ways I Have Hurt Others*

Reflect on the description you have written of your Messiah style and see if you can identify any instances in which you may have hurt others in similar fashion. Clearly describe how your attempts to help have been damaging. Write down names and specific examples.

Ways Carmen has hurt others:

I primarily hurt others through my arrogance. For example, Alan called me one night to talk about trouble he was having with his roommate. It was so clear to me that they were competing with each other. I could see that Alan had minimal confidence in himself. Instead of allowing Alan the chance to talk and sort that out for himself, I quickly pointed out that he had low self-esteem and was trying to establish his worth through conflict with his roommate. I also told him exactly what I thought he should say to his roommate. After dispensing this advice, I ended the conversation feeling that I had helped him immensely. I can now see that I had further undermined Alan's confidence by treating him as if he were incompetent. In addition, I hurt him by exposing his vulnerability, by telling him what to do, and by indirectly shaming him.

Ways I have hurt others:

Exercise 3:   *Identifying My Feelings Regarding My Harmful Actions*

Facing the fact that I have hurt another human being is, perhaps, the most difficult challenge I have ever faced. A number of feelings are stirred up inside of me. Select one of the situations described in the previous exercise and ponder it in more detail. Sit back for a few moments and allow your feelings to surface. Once you have experienced all the feelings you associate with this situation, write them or draw pictures of them below.

Carmen's feelings:

Sadness, remorse, humility, caring, guilt, desire to make amends.

My feelings:

Exercise 4:   *Asking God for Help*

In session 2 we discussed the concept of "false guilt" as a common experience for those of us caught in the Messiah Trap. In this session, however, we are identifying situations in which we are genuinely guilty.

As I take responsibility for my own actions, I am brought, again and again, to a place where I realize I can't make this recovery journey alone. I am in need of a Power greater than myself to grapple with the guilt, loss, shame, and other feelings I experience. Strength is needed to make amends. As I trust God to transform me, from the inside out, I can pray for healing. Then I become able to forgive myself as well as to ask for forgiveness from God and those I have harmed.

Facing the harm we have caused others is central to our recovery. As a testimony to the significance of this issue, seven of the Twelve Steps are devoted to addressing this very problem.

> Step 4: We made a searching and fearless moral inventory of ourselves.
> Step 5: Admitted to God, to ourselves, and to another human being the exact nature of our wrongs.
> Step 6: Were entirely ready to have God remove all these defects of character.
> Step 7: Humbly asked God to remove our shortcomings.
> Step 8: Made a list of all persons we had harmed, and became willing to make amends to them all.
> Step 9: Made direct amends to such people wherever possible, except when to do so would injure them or others.
> Step 10: Continued to take personal inventory and, when we were wrong, promptly admitted it.

In the following space, write out a prayer to your Higher Power, acknowledging the damage you have done. Many of us, because of unpleasant religious experience, feel stifled in our communication with God. I urge you to talk with your Higher Power as freely as you would any close friend. If it helps, imagine God in the way you did in previous sessions—as a dove, a fire, or a friend. In your own words, ask God to help you through this process and open yourself up to the healing and forgiveness that are available to you.

Carmen's prayer:

God, I can see that I have harmed Alan's sense of himself through my self-serving helping actions. I know that you love Alan and it hurts you when he hurts. I am very sorry about what I have done and ask for you to forgive me. I realize that my hurtful actions are rooted in my own distorted sense of myself. I consider myself more highly and less highly than is accurate. I open myself up to your healing and ask you to remove these shortcomings from my life. I will expect your continued guidance as I make my recovery journey. Last, I ask for insight and courage as I meet with Alan and apologize for what I have done. It is humbling to admit a failure. Help me to be honest and strong, willing to take responsibility for what I have done.

My prayer:

Recovery Ritual

Many religious rituals focus on the forgiveness of wrongdoing or the cleansing of past errors. Depending on your religious background, you may want to borrow ideas from these religious traditions. As we honor the process of confession and forgiveness, we more fully experience that, even though we are flawed, we are nevertheless lovable and acceptable.

Carmen's recovery ritual:

I will write Alan's name on a piece of paper and place it in my fireplace. I will light it and, as it burns, I will repeat the prayer I wrote to God. As the smoke ascends, I will visualize my guilt floating away from me. In its place, I will make room for an experience of peace and well-being.

My recovery ritual:

Admitting to
Another Human
Being the Exact
Nature of Our
Wrongs

Recovery Expression

Previously, the Recovery Expression has concentrated primarily on developing a stronger support network while selecting key persons with whom you could share your personal journey. Today's focus will differ, consisting of two parts. First, in keeping with Step 5, we will select someone with whom we can entrust a description of our harmful actions. Second, as indicated in Step 9, it is important to make amends whenever possible, except when to do so would injure those involved.

Step 1:
Selecting Who to Tell About My Personal Recovery Session

Because you have developed a stronger support network, there are a number of people who may be appropriate for selection. Disclosure of error can be a positive experience in the context of therapy or a support group. A close friend can also provide you with the support needed.

Select someone who has a forgiving heart. But also look for someone who won't minimize what you have done. Some people will try to "get you off the hook" rather than support you by holding you accountable for your actions. I recommend that you choose someone who is kind but firm, loving but not afraid of facing the truth, and forgiving rather than blaming.

The person Carmen will talk to about her wrongdoing:

My therapist

The person I will talk to about my wrongdoing:

Step 2:
Deciding What to Tell Others About My Recovery Session

As you ponder what you will share, be clear about what you want to accomplish. Admitting a wrong to another person is a way we help ourselves be honest with ourselves. I can lose sight of that fact and swing from one extreme to another. At times, I have described my wrongdoing in excessively horrible terms or severely minimized the impact. Distorting the truth undermines the goal of the exercise. Remember, sharing this information is to help you see yourself accurately. This person cannot "forgive" since the wrong deed does not involve him or her. Ask only for support and acceptance as you face this difficult part of the journey.

What Carmen will tell about her recovery session:

I will tell my therapist: I hurt a friend of mine by undermining his self-esteem. By acting like the expert, I treated him as if he were incompetent. I am so afraid he will leave me if he decides he doesn't need me. Instead of harming him, however, I want to learn how to care about him in genuinely helpful ways. For me to do so, I must first care for myself so that I come to believe I am lovable. I appreciate your listening to me talk about this. When you accept me, even though you know I am capable of hurting other people, I am more able to believe that I am acceptable and lovable.

What I will tell about my recovery session:

Making Direct
Amends to Such
People Whenever
Possible, Except
When to Do So
Would Injure
Them or Others

Step 1:
Selecting with Whom I Will Make Amends

One or more people may be involved in your wrongdoing. To the extent possible, include all affected parties. If you feel that making amends would be harmful, then omit this section. However, I urge you to be brutally honest with yourself about this. Making amends can be painful and an easy task to avoid. When at all possible, I recommend that you deal directly with those you have harmed so that deeper intimacy and caring can occur.

The person(s) to whom Carmen will make amends:

Alan

The person(s) to whom I will make amends:

Step 2:
Deciding What to Say About My Harmful Actions

Before you speak directly with the person or persons you have selected, carefully plan what you intend to say and prepare yourself for a variety of reactions. Some people will be open to your apology, and forgiveness will come easily. Others will become embarrassed and, in an attempt to avoid uncomfortable feelings, say something like, "Oh, that didn't bother me at all. No harm done." Still others will take the chance to blast you about everything you have ever done to upset them and maybe even ventilate anger they are feeling about someone else who hurt them recently. Preparing yourself for different reactions would be wise.

Reconciliation is easiest with those who are able to acknowledge that they have been hurt and yet are open to making amends. Often I feel initially relieved that I am not being excessively punished for my misdeed. Such an interaction is a wonderful gateway to genuine intimacy, however, and if I am not ready to move into a deeper, more caring relationship, I can soon feel uneasy again. I am best prepared when I acknowledge that intimacy does, in fact, scare me but I am willing to learn to be close without getting absorbed. Being aware of my feelings helps me in times of growth such as these.

The second group, consisting of those who minimize the situation, is a little more difficult. Here I am, after working up my courage, confessing to some wrongful deed and the person says, "No, you're wrong. You haven't hurt me." While this person may think he or she is doing me a favor by letting me off this way, it doesn't feel very good at the time. First, I am being told that my perceptions are off and I don't really know what occurred between us. Second, I feel exposed since I am out there apologizing for, apparently, no reason at all. In such cases, I tend to follow through on my apology anyway, saying something like, "Well, I don't need to make trouble for us if there is none, but it is my perception that I have behaved in violation of my own standards. The way I treated you was not the way I want to treat other people. While I am glad you were not hurt, I still want to acknowledge that I behaved in a manner unacceptable to me."

If the person was genuinely not harmed by my behavior, he or she usually sits quietly and accepts what I say kindly. Often, this person will take comfort in the fact that I am holding myself accountable in this manner. Should a felt misdeed occur in the future, my friend now knows that discussion would be welcome.

Most of the time, however, the person was actually hurt by my actions but wanted to avoid talking about it. By the time I finish my statement, it is common for the person to be more willing to risk admitting hurt. An opportunity for deeper intimacy results from my persistence.

Having a strategy for dealing with excessive anger is critical as we try to make amends with those we have harmed. The goal of making amends with someone is to promote deeper, more loving intimacy. It is not to create yet another situation in which we are abused. Since we Messiahs tend to be perfectionists, we can easily decide that if we erred at all, we are utter failures. We were good but now we are bad, and worthy of any punishment given.

To avoid abuse and promote safe intimacy, I recommend that you have a clear picture in your mind of exactly what you have done and just "how bad" it is. On a scale from one to ten, how would you rate this misdeed? Is it a two? a seven? an all-out ten?

In keeping with this rating, what is an appropriate response from the wronged party? Irritation? Annoyance? Rage?

Have a clear picture of what is acceptable to you. If the person begins to bring up other instances of similar behavior, exaggerates the current situation, or becomes irrational, I urge you to terminate the conversation. You can say, for example, "I am not ready to apologize for every time I have hurt you, just this one time. I am not willing to discuss this any further with you." Never feel obligated to endure abuse, verbal or physical, as a part of making amends. Taking responsibility for the harm you have done does not include passively submitting yourself to harm.

What Carmen will say in making amends:

Alan, I want to talk to you about our conversation last week regarding your roommate. As I have thought about this, I realize that I did not live up to my own standards as a friend. My intention was to be supportive and helpful, but it seems to me that, instead, I acted like an expert and treated you disrespectfully. Only you know what really goes on between you and your roommate and so only you can be the final judge of what is best. As an outsider, my opinion may be helpful, but I feel like I pushed it on you rather than offered it as a gift. I do have faith in you and am very sorry that I did not communicate that very well. I am sorry for what I have done and for any harm you have suffered. I would like you to forgive me.

What I will say in making amends:

Recovery Celebration

Phew! If we ever needed to celebrate it is now! What a tough session this has been . . . and an exciting one as new opportunities for healing and intimacy become possible. Perhaps you would like to include in your celebration the person with whom you just made amends. This could be a wonderful way to solidify the gains made in the relationship.

I recommend that you discuss together various ways to celebrate your deepening relationship. Perhaps you have a special place the two of you like to visit. Or maybe you share a special song and will celebrate by dancing in the living room. If you have no traditions yet, this may be the perfect time to start one! How about getting a frozen yogurt at the local ice cream parlor? Having brunch at the new café in town? Flying a kite in the park? Going window-shopping? You have already deepened your relationship through painful and courageous work. I urge you to also take the opportunity to deepen your relationships through celebration.

If your overture of making amends was not well received, you have all the more need for celebration. Rather than celebrate a desired outcome, you can celebrate your courage and dedication to your own recovery, regardless of the obstacles. We all experience disappointment. You are not strange or odd, if you weren't understood or forgiven as you wanted. I urge you to call a trusted friend and invite him or her to celebrate with you, thereby deepening intimacy with someone else, someone who is able and willing to accept you as you are.

Recovery Checklist

- ☐ I initiated the session with a recovery ritual
- ☐ I read pages 56–72 in *When Helping You Is Hurting Me* and the Twelve Steps
- ☐ I identified ways my Messiah style hurts others
- ☐ I identified ways I have hurt others
- ☐ I identified my feelings regarding my harmful actions
- ☐ I asked God for help
- ☐ I created a recovery ritual
- ☐ I selected who to tell about my recovery session
- ☐ I selected what to say about my recovery session
- ☐ I selected with whom I would make amends
- ☐ I selected what to say about my harmful actions
- ☐ I celebrated my progress

 Conclude the session with your recovery ritual.

Session 10

I Am Ready for Love

Accepting Love and Nurturance

I used to believe that love was a scarce commodity that had been dispersed long before I showed up. Satisfaction was a feeling unknown to me, while longing and deprivation were familiar companions. The Messiah Trap had convinced me that there was not enough love in the world for me, not now, not ever. It would always be someone else's turn.

Now I see that there is plenty of what I need, and enough not only for me but for everyone else as well. There is enough self-esteem in this world for everyone to feel valued. Safety is available in such abundance that no one need be in fear again. There is ample nurturance for everyone to be nourished. And love? There is enough love for every person on the planet to experience the attention and caring that he or she deserves and needs.

Why was I deprived for so many years? In fact, why do I still experience periods of deprivation if there is plenty available? Simply stated, I believe that I have a limited ability to accept what I need. I have been impaired by the lies of the Messiah Trap to such a degree that I am unable to eat the feast that God brings to my table.

Those of us caught in the Messiah Trap see life from a perspective of scarcity. Since there doesn't seem to be enough for everyone, hard choices must be made to determine who must suffer deprivation or abuse. We Messiahs have been trained to sacrifice ourselves so that others can have what they need. We give but do not receive. We sacrifice but our efforts do not result in rebirth. The real tragedy is exposed when we realize that the sacrifices we make to the god of our addiction are unnecessary.

Furthermore, our sacrifices are futile, because as we saw more clearly in the last session, people are not helped and may actually be harmed by our addictive helping.

When we clear our minds of the Messiah lies, our eyes are opened to the abundance available. When we let go of the Messiah Trap, our hands are freed to embrace those who love us. In the context of balanced love, we give and receive. Our sacrifices are redeemed as doorways into a new, more loving reality.

You may be asking, "Where is the place of abundance? It's just the same old world of pain and struggle, as far as I can see." In this session we will look at the spiral process of accepting love and nurturance into our lives, wherein we, step by step, travel into an abundant land.

Recovery Reading

The recommended reading: the section entitled "Learn to Accept Love and Nurturance," pages 97–100, in *When Helping You Is Hurting Me.*

Recovery Reflection

When I hide behind my Messiah mask, I can pretend that I am a great lover of humanity. "Look at all my great efforts," I arrogantly say to the world. "I am busy every day in the care of others." But if I pull off that mask and look honestly at myself and my relationships, I am forced to admit that I am a novice when it comes to love. Consider me an expert on guilt and fear. I know all about deprivation, obligation, and pain. But love? No, loving is something I know very little about.

Throughout this workbook I have emphasized that no one can escape the Messiah Trap alone. We all need one another. Our ability to love others is dependent upon the love we have received. Similarly, our ability to receive love is dependent upon our capacity to give love to others.

Each phase of this cycle builds upon the other. The more love we are able to receive, the more we are changed and the more we are able to love others. The more we are able to love others, the more we are able to receive love in return. The process of growth is one of "give and receive," not "give and give and give and give until you have nothing left" as we experienced in the Messiah Trap.

If this is a cyclical process, where do I start learning? How do I get this carousel to slow down so I can jump on?

I believe the initial step in learning to give love is learning to receive love. I used to judge my caring by how much I gave to or did for another person. But now I realize that a more accurate assessment of my love is this: I love someone to the extent that I allow that person to make a difference in my life.*

As I receive other persons into my life and accept their love for me, I am changed. By receiving love, my capacity to love in return is expanded. I have more love to give to others. When they receive my love, they, in turn, experience an increased capacity to love. They have more love to give to me, which then serves to increase my capacity for healthy caring.

What a different picture this is from the one-sided intimacy I experienced while in the Messiah Trap! I gave but felt I had no right to receive. Instead of experiencing a growing capacity to care, what little I had was bled dry. My garden was overgrown with choking weeds while my fruit-bearing plants withered and died. I did not know how to receive nourishment from others.

What keeps me from receiving the love and nurturance I so desperately want? I believe that several obstacles stand between me and the love that is available to me. First, when I am caught in the Messiah Trap, I am busy trying to earn love rather than receive love. Under my smiling, helping exterior is a demanding neediness that grabs at people and, in fact, scares them away. Second, since my focus is on getting other people to give me what I want, I am blind to the ways I am able to receive the genuine love that is being offered to me. I do not know myself well enough to recognize which expressions of love are actually nurturing to me. Third, I do not ask directly for what I want or

---

*Carmen Berry and Mark Taylor, *Loving Yourself as Your Neighbor* (San Francisco: Harper & Row, 1990).

Escaping the Messiah Trap

need because I am afraid my request will be refused. It is easier for me to be covert rather than honest about my needs. Fourth, I do not invite people to express their love for me because I am afraid others will come too close or hurt me in some way. And last, since I am used to looking for love in all the wrong places, I am unable to recognize love when it is freely given. We will address each of these obstacles in the following exercises.

Exercise 1:   *Letting Go of My Efforts to Earn Love*

I often experience feelings of deprivation. Instead of using my energy to enlarge my ability to receive love and nurturance, however, I get sidetracked by the Messiah Trap. I try to earn love by doing "helpful" things for others. The problem with this approach is simple. It doesn't work. I have never successfully convinced someone to love me who didn't want to love me. Unable to see that I am being secretly manipulative, I soon feel angry and resentful. Thoughts go through my mind such as, "After all I have done for other people, why can't any of them attend to me?" and "I am always unappreciated by my friends. They owe me." I may never say these thoughts aloud, but it is easy for me to feel entitled to nurturance from particular people in a manner of my choosing.

When free of the Messiah Trap, I realize that no one owes me anything. No one has the right to abuse me, but at the same time, no one is obligated to love me. Love is a gift that is freely given. If someone does not choose to love me, that is his or her right. Only those people who choose to care about me and commit themselves to my nurturance have a responsibility to follow through on their promises. As I look over my past relationships, I must be honest and admit that I prefer to be the one who determines who loves me and what they offer me. When in the Messiah Trap, I want control.

Describe a current relationship in which you want more than you are receiving. Are you feeling resentful toward this person because you feel you are not getting what you want or need from him or her? Are you, as I do so often, trying to control, manipulate, or otherwise "make" the person love you and give you what you want? Are you feeling resentful, deprived, and entitled to more? What are you doing to try to get this person to do what you want?

Ways Carmen is trying to "make" someone love and nurture her:

I met a man whom I found attractive. As we talked, I tried to figure out things he might need that I could give. I listened for hours as he talked about various concerns and problems, but he never initiated a date. I was hoping that if he came to depend on me, he would ask me out. When he didn't ask me out, I became resentful.

Ways I am trying to "make " someone love and nurture me:

To make room for people who choose to love and nurture us, we must first let go of self-defeating expectations and unnurturing relationships. The relationship we have just described is one in which we want more love and nurturance than the person is currently willing to give. Quite honestly, our creativity is being wasted on this relationship. We would be better served to accept what this person is offering while letting go of our efforts to manipulate, control, coerce, seduce, or otherwise make that person give us what we need.

In previous sessions, we have used visualization to help us "let go." I often use the hot air balloon visualization, wherein I place my relationship and expectations into the basket of the balloon and let it rise out of sight behind the clouds. Use whatever method seems to work best for you and let go of the unrealistic expectations held for this relationship. Make room for someone new or for a new beginning in this relationship by letting go of the current focus on control.

Carmen's method of letting go:

I will walk to a nearby Japanese garden and sit quietly by myself. I will reflect on the many aspects of this relationship: what I had expected from the relationship, what I have received, what I have not received, and how I have tried to make this person love and nurture me. After I have fully contemplated the situation, I will visualize my offering this relationship to God. I will visualize God's hands coming down through the clouds and taking this relationship from me. I will release this relationship and my unmet expectations to the care of my Higher Power.

My method of letting go:

Exercise 2:   *Identifying Ways I Receive Love and Nurturance*

Since we are all human, we all have legitimate needs for love and nurturance. However, since we are also individuals, we differ in the ways we are able to receive and enjoy the nurturance offered to us. Some people feel loved when they are allowed space to pursue their own interests. Others enjoy being held closely. Some want to hear the words "I love you," while others want to be shown through acts of kindness. We must become acquainted with ourselves so that we know how we are currently able to receive love and nurturance and how we would like to expand this ability.

What are the ways you are currently able to receive nurturance into your life? How is love most convincingly expressed to you? After which experiences do you feel satisfied and nourished?

In the following space, identify the various ways you receive love and nurturance. You may want to write a list, draw pictures, or make a collage of magazine photos depicting situations, experiences, or items that are nurturing to you. These could include scenes of family gatherings, friends sharing a cup of coffee, or romantic kisses between lovers. Experiences that are nurturing to you may come to you through your body—for example, touching, dancing, sailing, bike riding, or taking a stroll. You may feel loved by someone if you are given flowers, a back massage, or a favorite CD. Take some time with this exercise and identify the ways you are able to receive nurturance at the present time.

Ways Carmen receives love and nurturance:

1. *Being listened to when I need to talk*
2. *Being allowed time alone when I need to think things through on my own*
3. *Receiving a massage*
4. *Walking in the garden with someone I enjoy*
5. *Receiving small gifts such as cards, flowers, and books as expressions of caring*

6. Relaxing with someone I trust
7. Enjoying a weekend away
8. Hearing a compliment
9. Being held
10. Sharing jokes and laughter

Ways I receive love and nurturance:

Look over the ways you receive love and nurturance and ponder these questions:

- Am I able to receive love in a wide variety of ways, or just two or three?
- How difficult was this exercise for me? Am I aware of the ways I can receive love or is receiving love a mystery to me?
- How can I develop more ways to receive love and nurturance?
- How often do I actually receive love and nurturance in the ways described?

In this exercise I wrote that I receive nurturance through taking a walk with a friend. Even though this is one of the ways I feel loved, I must admit that I haven't gone for a walk with someone in months. I deprive myself of nurturance when I deprive myself of those experiences that nurture me. When I ask a friend to go for a walk with me, I open myself more fully to the love that is available. As you review your list, you may also find you have experienced only a few, if any, of the nurturing situations described. How long has it been since you had a professional massage? When did you last ride your bike or go to the gym? How have you nurtured your body? If you love to go on spiritual retreats, when did you last get away for a weekend? What about a romantic interlude? Provide for yourself access to these experiences. It is your responsibility to open yourself up to love and nurturance.

Perhaps most of your effort has been put into getting love "indirectly," through addictive helping activities. Instead of trying to obligate people to love you through "helping," I recommend a more direct approach: Learn to ask for what you need.

Exercise 3:   ### Learning to Ask for What I Need by Facing the Fear of Rejection

I'll admit, it is very difficult for me to acknowledge that I am a human being, like everyone else. It is even more difficult for me to look someone in the eye and ask him or her to help meet my legitimate needs. Even though I have gotten more proficient at asking for what I need, I can still feel a shiver go down my spine at the thought of such vulnerability. What if I gather up the courage to ask for what I need and am told no? Ugh. It's almost too awful to imagine.

Think back to a situation in which you risked telling someone what you needed and felt rejected and deprived. Describe that situation below.

A situation in which Carmen asked someone for what she needed but still felt rejected and deprived:

I was upset about a problem at work and needed to talk about it. I went over to see a friend of mine and asked if I could talk to her about it. She

said okay and I started talking. I was very upset and wanted to express how angry I was. Before I was finished describing what had happened, she tried to give me advice. That made me angry. I just wanted her to listen. I kept talking and soon she started looking at the clock. That hurt my feelings. I though to myself, "I listen whenever she needs to talk." I abruptly got up and left, feeling rejected and embarrassed for being vulnerable. I went home depressed because I was still upset about my work problem, but now I was also angry at my friend.

A situation in which I asked someone for what I needed but felt rejected and deprived:

Rejection and disappointment are experiences we all would like to avoid. I have learned several skills that have helped to minimize my encounters with rejection. First, it is important for me to be clear on what I need and to be able to state this need in measurable terms. If I come to another person expecting that person to "fix" me, to undo all the damage I've experienced, to make up for all my losses, to make me feel loved when I don't love myself, then, of course, I will be disappointed. No one human being has infinite resources to heal my interior wounds. But if I clearly state that I need something specific, something defined and having boundaries, I am more likely to receive and experience realistic satisfaction.

Review the situation you described above. Did you ask for exactly what you needed or did you expect the other person to read your mind? Were you clear on what you needed?

Describe what you needed in measurable terms. Here are some examples:

Nonmeasurable	Measurable
I needed acceptance, not advice.	I needed someone to listen to me for one hour.
I needed to have some fun.	I needed to go out dancing on Friday night.
I needed space.	I needed the afternoon to myself.

What Carmen needed:

I needed someone to listen to me. If I honestly assess how upset I was and how much I needed to talk, I would say that I could have talked for two and a half hours about this problem.

What I needed:

Now that our needs have been clearly identified, we move to the task of opening ourselves up to those who are offering to love and nurture us. I have learned that no one person or relationship sufficiently meets my needs. When in the Messiah Trap, I tend to place unrealistic expectations on one relationship and ask this person to meet all my needs. Even if my selected person initially wants to nurture me, he or she will eventually tire and pull away. Whether this person is polite or rude, kind or harsh, I feel rejected. Not only do I feel deprived, having my original need unmet, I now feel embarrassed, angry, and disappointed for exposing my need.

After trial and error, I have learned to utilize several relationships in order to get my needs met. For example, if I have a situation needing considerable attention, I ask several friends for time to talk. I also take the problem to my support group and discuss it in therapy as well. In addition, I ask God for assistance and receive nurturance through prayer. I am also learning to love and nurture myself better, so I process part of the problem through writing in a journal, active imagination, meditation, drawing, and dance. Eventually, I receive my two and a half hours of nurturance but I haven't overly stressed any one relationship. I come away feeling loved by several people rather than rejected by one. Using the same need identified above, develop a plan wherein you could ask several people to help meet your need.

People Carmen will ask to help meet her need:

I will talk with my therapist for one hour, call three close friends and talk for twenty minutes to each, go to my support group and talk for five minutes, call the man in my life and talk for twenty-five minutes. I get two and a half hours of support without overly stressing any one person.

People I will ask to help meet my need:

Exercise 4:   *Creating Safety So That I Am Free to Invite Others Closer*

One of the primary reasons we Messiahs hide behind our helping roles is to avoid further pain. We have all been hurt by other people and we are making valiant efforts to keep ourselves safe. Unfortunately, when we keep ourselves safe the Messiah way, we also find ourselves painfully isolated.

As we turn toward intimacy, our fear of hurt stops us short. How do we create safe boundaries between ourselves and others so that, if they do come closer to us, they don't come too close? What if we let our barriers down and are then defenseless to purposeful or unintentional harm from others?

In the last exercise, we discussed skills that can help us minimize our risk of rejection. These skills can also help us better protect ourselves from becoming inappropriately vulnerable to other people. We most often experience hurt from others when we misjudge a situation and, therefore, neglect to protect ourselves. As Messiahs, we have tried to protect ourselves by being "good" or pleasing others. Our attention is focused on how other people feel, while we ignore how we feel. Our own bodies, feelings, and thoughts continually signal us to danger, yet because of our addiction, we ignore these signals.

Having realistic expectations for ourselves and others is the greatest weapon we have against abuse. When we see things clearly, we can then take the proper protective actions.

Describe a situation in which you recently felt unsafe, in danger, or actually harmed by another person. Perhaps you invited someone in closer but soon felt suffocated or invaded. Maybe someone you trusted hurt you in a way you didn't expect and for which you were unprepared.

A situation in which Carmen felt unsafe or hurt:

I was working on a committee and volunteered to help the chairwoman. We stayed after the meeting to talk; later that week I heard that she twisted my words in a way that made me sound unprofessional.

A situation in which I felt unsafe or hurt:

Review the situation you described above. Did you ask for exactly what you needed or did you expect the other person to read your mind? Were you clear on what you needed?

Describe what you needed in measurable terms. Here are some examples:

Nonmeasurable

I felt physically invaded.

I felt emotionally invaded.

I felt hurt.

Measurable

I needed to sit in my own chair, not on his lap.

I needed my privacy and am not obligated to tell my mother everything about my new boyfriend.

I need my friend to express her feelings of anger calmly, not call me names or threaten me.

What Carmen needed:

I needed her to keep our conversation confidential.

What I needed:

Write out what you can say to this person to inform him or her of what you need. Do not blame or criticize. Avoid acting like a victim. Instead, clearly state what you need and hold the line. The more exact you can be when expressing what you need, the more likely others will be able to respond.

If someone refuses to listen or respond to your need for safety, it is important to prune this person out of your life. You have no obligation to keep an abusive, insensitive, or intrusive person in your life. Remember, love is a gift, not an obligation. No one is obligated to love you or me. And we are not obligated to love other people. None of us has the right to hurt another person, but love is a free choice.

Exercise 5:   ***Recognizing Love When It Is Freely Given***

We Messiahs look for love in all the wrong places from people who are unwilling or unable to nurture us. As we break free of our addiction, however, we can learn to see love in places we previously overlooked. As a Messiah, I have developed 20/20 vision for sadness, pain, loss, and grief. I can spot a person in trouble the second I enter a room. But I have to develop the ability to locate those around me who were able and willing to love me.

Are you able to recognize love when it is offered to you? I have often been blind to the gifts of love offered to me. In hindsight, I have realized the many missed opportunities. For example, in my addictive fervor, I did not return the phone call from a friend asking me out to lunch. She didn't need me to help her, she just wanted to enjoy being with me. I didn't know what to say when there was no problem to discuss, so I pulled away. People have tried to offer me more love than I could receive.

Stop for a moment and think over the past couple of weeks. Who has offered you love? I have no doubt, regardless of how neglected you may feel at the moment, that someone in the recent past has reached out to you and you looked the other way. What about the friend who left a message on your machine two weeks ago? What about the co-worker who asked you to go to lunch but you chose to eat at your desk so you could get more work done? Didn't you receive a card from your aunt, asking how you've been doing lately? What about that "boring" man who keeps calling you for a date? Is he really boring or does he like you and that feels uncomfortable? Didn't your wife nuzzle up to you last night and you brushed her off?

Describe one situation in which you overlooked the love and nurturance offered.

A situation in which Carmen overlooked the love and nurturance offered:

A friend offered to take me to lunch just to be supportive. But I was so busy I did not respond.

A situation in which I overlooked the love and nurturance offered:

Make a commitment to yourself to have your eyes wide open for future offers of love and nurturance. As I have opened my eyes for love and nurturance, I have been delightfully surprised at how many opportunities are offered to me on a regular basis. Many people have expressed concern to me that, if they left the Messiah Trap behind, they would become selfish people who cared nothing for the needs of others. In fact, quite the opposite is true. When we escape the Trap, with its lies and deceit, we are free at last to genuinely love one another. Intimacy is possible for the first time in our lives. Love and nurturance, shared, not hoarded, are available to all. There is no scarcity. Love, as it is, is enough.

Recovery Ritual

Review today's exercises and select the aspect that was most meaningful for you. Develop a ritual that signifies the progress you have made today. You may want to create a ritual that honors your letting go of a nonloving relationship. This could be done by gathering together letters and other mementos that remind you of this relationship. After you place them in an appropriate container (perhaps by tying them up in a sack), they can be disposed of in the trash. By doing so, you have symbolically made room for a truly loving and nurturing relationship to come into your life.

On the other hand, you may want to focus on your increasing sense of safety and self-protective skill. You might draw a picture of yourself with soft but adequate armor. If you have been frightened, you may want to imagine yourself in a safe room with an unbreakable lock on the door. Create a symbol of safety for yourself to honor the fact that we can only experience healthy intimacy in the context of safety.

You may want to honor a deeper awareness that love and nurturance are in abundance. You could write out your commitment to accepting love and nurturance more fully in your life and keep this piece of paper in your wallet. This could serve as a constant reminder that you are lovable and open to nurturance.

Recovery Expression

Throughout this workbook, we have developed deeper intimacy with other people. This session is another opportunity to open yourself up to more of the love you legitimately need. Look over the exercises in this session and select the area in which you have the most need. As you do, select one relationship in which to deal with this issue. These are some examples:

1. Do you need to let go of expectations regarding a particular relationship? Talk to this person and clarify specific limitations, expectations, and boundaries.
2. Are you depriving yourself of nurturing experiences? Contact someone you love and arrange for a fresh opportunity to nurture each other.
3. Are you refusing to ask for what you need for fear of rejection? Select several friends and individually ask for what you need. Give yourself the opportunity to have all the support you require.
4. Do you need to create a safer context for yourself so that you are free to invite people closer? Talk with the person with whom you feel unsafe and set new boundaries for yourself.
5. Are you genuinely open to the love offered? Make that phone call. Write that note. Respond to those people who want to love you.

Step 1:
Selecting Who to Tell About My Recovery Session

The person Carmen will talk to about her recovery session:

A female friend who has expressed interest in spending more time with me.

The person I will talk to about my recovery session:

Step 2:
Deciding What to Tell Others About My Recovery Session

What Carmen will say about her recovery session:

I realized in today's recovery session that one of the reasons I feel deprived of nurturance is because I have overlooked gifts of love offered to me. Because of my hectic schedule I have not accepted any of your invitations to get together. I appreciate your interest in developing our relationship and I intend to be more available in the future.

What I will say about my recovery session:

Recovery Celebration

We have traveled a long way together over the past ten sessions. Your courage and persistence are impressive. Not only have you much to celebrate in this one session, you have opportunity to give honor to the work we have accomplished together.

Why not throw a party? As you have worked through this workbook, you have deepened your relationships. If you started attending a support group, you may now have friends you didn't even know when you started this journey. Since these people shared your pain and your progress, why not invite them to share in the celebration? They might enjoy meeting one another!

Have a great time. You deserve it. After all . . . *it's your turn!*

Recovery Checklist

☐ I initiated the session with a recovery ritual
☐ I read pages 97–100 in *When Helping You Is Hurting Me*
☐ I let go of my efforts to earn love
☐ I identified ways to receive love
☐ I asked for what I needed by facing my fear of rejection
☐ I created safety so I could invite others closer
☐ I recognized love when it is freely given
☐ I created a recovery ritual
☐ I selected who to tell about my recovery session
☐ I decided what to say about my recovery session
☐ I celebrated my progress

 Conclude the session with your recovery ritual.

Continuing the Journey

Coming to the end of this workbook need not indicate the end of your personal recovery sessions. Each session has six sections. You can use this model to create additional sessions. You can continue to initiate each session with your established recovery ritual and then follow the plan outlined below.

Recovery Reading

The recovery field is bursting with new, helpful information on a wide variety of recovery issues. Select a book of interest to you and read a chapter or small portion to serve as a focus for the session.

Recovery Reflection

Reflect upon the reading to ascertain how this new information can be applied to your interior life. You have participated in various exercises in this workbook that can be adapted or modified to new topics. Exercises include writing descriptions of past experiences, drawing pictures of your interior reality, and dancing your feelings. You learned recovery techniques such as meditation, visualization, and active imagination. By applying your creativity to the exercises and techniques in this workbook, you can enhance and continue your journey.

Recovery Ritual

By now you are adept at creating recovery rituals to honor your interior progress. After all, you created at least ten of these rituals in this workbook. A ritual is a symbolic way to bridge the gap between the interior and the exterior. I highly recommend that you include ritual in your regular recovery journey.

Recovery Expression

Love is the goal as well as the means of our recovery. We want to love ourselves, God, and others more deeply. To learn to love, we must risk opening ourselves up to others. Select at least one person to share what you have learned in each session in order to deepen intimacy and solidify your personal growth.

Recovery Celebration

The recovery process can be extremely painful. Unless we make a conscious effort, the joy of life can seem like a future dream, not a present reality. By creating a recovery celebration for each session, you will bring more happiness into your present life, lessen the pain of the process, and reward yourself for a job well done.

Recovery Checklist

List specifically what you have accomplished in each session. I am always surprised when I do this because I find I have made so much more progress than I realized. This recovery checklist is another way to honor yourself as the courageous and committed person that you are.

It has been a privilege to walk with you on this journey of recovery. As you continue to do the work that will heal you and bring fulfillment into your life, I hope others can celebrate your progress with you. Remember that you are not alone. There are many of us on this journey, and we can all take strength from the fact that the path is not a solitary one.

Appendix A

The Twelve Steps*

1. We admitted we were powerless over our addiction—that our lives had become unmanageable.

2. Came to believe that a Power greater than ourselves could restore us to sanity.

3. Made a decision to turn our will and our lives over to the care of God *as we understood God.*

4. Made a searching and fearless moral inventory of ourselves.

5. Admitted to God, to ourselves, and to another human being the exact nature of our wrongs.

6. Were entirely ready to have God remove all these defects of character.

7. Humbly asked God to remove our shortcomings.

8. Made a list of all persons we had harmed, and became willing to make amends to them all.

9. Made direct amends to such people wherever possible, except when to do so would injure them or others.

10. Continued to take personal inventory and, when we were wrong, promptly admitted it.

11. Sought through prayer and meditation to improve our conscious contact with God, . . . praying only for knowledge of God's will for us and the power to carry that out.

12. Having had a spiritual awakening as the result of these steps, we tried to carry this message to others and to practice these principles in all our affairs.

---

*The Twelve Steps are reprinted and adapted with permission of Alcoholics Anonymous World Services, Inc. Permission to reprint and adapt the Twelve Steps does not mean that AA has reviewed or approved the contents of this publication, nor that AA agrees with the views expressed herein. AA is a program of recovery from alcoholism. Use of the Twelve Steps in connection with programs and activities which are patterned after AA but which address other problems does not imply otherwise. The Twelve Steps of Alcoholics Anonymous are reprinted in full on page 174.

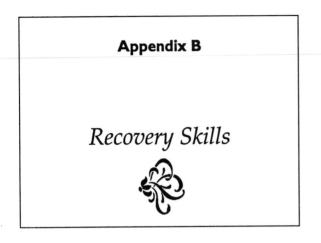

Appendix B

Recovery Skills

Skill 1: Securing a Support Group

What do you need from a recovery support group? This is an important question that you can systematically answer by exploring what your specific needs are and what kind of support group may be best suited for you. I believe we all need a "safe place." But what does that mean for you? What makes a group safe or unsafe for you? Over the years I have come to recognize that I need several things from a support group.

1. Anonymity

I need to attend a group where my confidentiality is protected. We Messiahs have worked hard at creating roles for ourselves that cause others to look up to us. When we come to a support group, we all need the chance to be one of the crowd, to be loved because we are there, not because we perform.

I have found that attending a support group that upholds confidentiality and anonymity provides me with the safe place I need. Perhaps you also live or work in a situation that makes honest disclosure dangerous. Perhaps discussing problems and failures could actually mean the loss of your job and financial security. Finding a safe place where your identity is protected, then, is one of the things needed.

2. Leadership

Over the years I have found that I am most comfortable in groups that function without needing my leadership. When I first began my recovery, I set up my own "Messiahs Anonymous" group. If you live in an area where there are no appropriate support groups, perhaps you will want to start such a group yourself.

I found, for myself, however, that I needed a place where I was not looked to as a leader. It was important for me to feel free to attend to my own needs and issues without worrying about whether the chairs were set up, the coffee was made, or the building was locked up at the end of each meeting.

3. Group Structure

I believe that support groups of all types can be helpful if properly executed. Some groups allow cross talk, which is another term for "discussion." People can share deeply about how they feel in a discussion group. Many support groups are structured around the discussion model.

There is a special danger in groups that allow cross talk, however, because we can be tempted to turn our focus away from our own growth and onto finding solutions for other people's problems. I have attended recovery discussion groups and have been greatly helped, as long as I am constantly aware of my tendency to fall back into my addiction. I find myself pretending to be an expert rather than a regular member.

Groups that disallow cross talk can be extremely helpful for those of us trying to escape the Messiah Trap. These groups are perhaps the safest for those of us addicted to helping. Groups structured in this manner, which include most Anonymous groups, give members the chance to share deeply and intimately about their journeys. The group listens attentively and supportively. But no one is expected to "fix" anyone else. Each member is expected to sort through his or her own situation and, with the support of the group and God's help, decide what is the proper course of action.

4. Privacy

A fourth area that is important to me is privacy. I have been in groups where enormous pressure was put on members to "spill their guts." Such a group is dangerous and inappropriate for those of us in recovery. It is of utmost importance to me that my privacy be respected and honored. Consequently, I need a group that allows me to do whatever is most helpful to me, whether that be to talk or to sit quietly. I especially enjoy my Anonymous Twelve-Step group because there is never any pressure for me to do anything that feels uncomfortable. I feel fully supported when I decide to share with the group, and loved and nurtured on the nights that I sit quietly, deep inside my own thoughts.

These are some of the things I need from a support group. You may want to list specifically what you need from a support group.

What I need from a support group:

Identifying Obstacles to Attending a Support Group

Asking for help may be difficult. I don't like asking for help and especially don't like asking for help from people I don't know. It is easy for me to come up with a long list of reasons why attending a support group is not for me. Some of the obstacles I have constructed are listed below.

1. I don't have the time. With all my responsibilities, I'm lucky to get one hour a week to do this recovery workbook. How could I find the time to attend a group every week?

2. I don't need help; I'm not in that bad a shape. I just have a little problem with helping, that's all.

3. I'm all alone. I won't know anyone there. I'm too embarrassed to go alone. It's just too scary going to a group by myself.

My obstacles:

Overcoming Obstacles to Attending a Support Group

It is hard for us Messiahs to nurture ourselves. We feel obligated to take care of everyone else before we attend to our own needs. Our lifestyles are structured so that every hour is allocated to helping someone other than ourselves. Changing our priorities to include ourselves can be quite a challenge.

To help you remember how important it is to make a safe place for yourself, I urge you to review session 1. Remember how hard it was to find one hour a week for yourself to do these workbook sessions? And yet now, it is a regular part of your routine. Finding the time to attend a support group will be a similar process. It was helpful for me to discover that these support groups meet at a variety of times—some in the morning, some in the afternoon, and some in the evening. There are meetings during the workweek and also on the weekends. There is a group for every kind of schedule. At first it may be difficult to make the time for a weekly group, but once you and your friends and family adjust to your new routine, things will settle down into a regular pace. You may want to review the exercises in session 1 to help you tell those in your life about this new phase in your recovery journey.

If you are feeling guilty about taking more time for yourself, I urge you to remind yourself that it is finally time to *take your turn*.

Like me, you may try to avoid getting help by pretending your problems aren't all that bad. Denial is something with which all addicts struggle. Alcoholics can be passed out in the gutter and still proclaim with full confidence that they are not out of control with their drinking. We addicts can look reality in the eye and still ignore its existence.

At certain points during the recovery process, we will be tempted to deny the extent to which we are addicted. My denial is usually triggered at moments when I am faced with doing something new, something that may frighten me. I say to myself, "Hey, wait a minute now. Let's take this one slowly. Maybe I'm not as bad off as all that. I'd rather go back to what is familiar than try this new thing."

If you are tempted, at this point, to tell yourself that you do not need to attend a support group, I urge you to remember how much pain you have been feeling, the losses you have experienced because of this addiction. We all need help and support. If you are caught in the Messiah Trap, you need support like the rest of us.

Another obstacle to getting help is fear of the unknown. Thinking about going to a group, where you may not know anyone, could be a frightening prospect. I suspect there may be some concerns or fears connected to going to a support group, especially if you have never attended such a group.

When I am the leader of a group, I feel very confident and can walk up and talk to anyone. But when I do not have a specific role, I can feel lost and shy. It is hard for me to walk into a room of strangers when by myself. I feel self-conscious and awkward, wondering where I should sit or with whom I should talk.

To help me take that first step into a new group, I often invite a friend to go with me. Sometimes I already know a person in the group and ask that person to meet me a few minutes before the meeting starts. We can then walk in together. If I know no one in the group, I may find someone who is also interested in checking out this particular group. I have even asked a friend to go with me as a onetime support effort. Once I attend a group and get to know the routine and the people, it is much easier for me to attend the next week on my own.

Taking those initial steps is the hardest for me. You may have other fears or concerns. You may feel very shy in any type of group. Talking to strangers about your problems may seem frightening. On the other hand, you may be quite outgoing and fearless in group settings, but you are deceiving yourself into thinking that you don't really need a group to help you. Please honestly assess your feelings and thoughts to identify any obstacles you may be constructing to keep yourself from getting the support you actually need.

Remember, *no one escapes the Messiah Trap alone.* Be brutally honest with yourself now. You may be sabotaging your recovery by coming up with reasons why you don't need or can't deal with becoming a part of a support group.

Once you have made a commitment to select and attend a recovery support group, the next step is to develop a plan of action. I recommend that you attend several different groups before deciding to settle into any particular support group.

Collecting a List of Support Groups

A wide variety of support groups are available for those of us dealing with issues of codependency. Among the ways to develop your list are the ones I have listed.

1. Ask your friends about support groups they may attend or know about
2. Look in the phone book
3. Call the operator for special information numbers in your area
4. Check with a local mental health or treatment center
5. Look through the directories kept at your local library

Your friends may be a great source of information. In fact, I was amazed to find out how many of my friends and colleagues were attending support groups. Once I started asking around, I learned about several helpful groups.

You may also find a listing in the yellow pages and white pages of your phone book. These groups may be under headings such as "Alcoholism," "Adult Children of Alcoholics," "Codependency," "Counseling," and "Mental Health Services." If you have an additional addiction, such as an addiction to overeating, to sex, to gambling, or to relationships, you may also find support groups under these headings.

In some communities, an information and referral service is available. You may try calling the operator and asking if there is such a number in your area. Many mental health clinics and treatment centers keep a directory of support groups in their area. Another source may be the local library, where phone books and directories of all types are maintained.

Since the Twelve-Step model was originally developed to deal with alcoholism, many support groups emphasize alcohol-related problems. I have attended an Adult Children of Alcoholics (ACA) support group even though there is no alcoholism in my immediate family. I found that the issues ACAs struggle with are very similar to my struggles with the Messiah Trap.

While I do not think that the Twelve-Step groups are the only helpful support groups, I recommend groups structured around that model. Those of us who struggle with codependency have needs that may go beyond what the Twelve Steps can offer. However, groups that honor individual responsibility for personal growth, as do most Twelve-Step groups, can be very helpful to us Messiahs.

My list of recovery support groups:

Group	Meeting Time	Contact Person	Phone

Visiting and Assessing Recovery Support Groups

Now that you have a list of available support groups in your area, it is important to call the contact persons to get initial information. Use your list of what you need from a support group as a guideline as you interview the contact person for each group. You can eliminate any group from your list if you are told that the group is set up in a way that does not meet your needs.

Once you have talked with each contact person to see if the group is structured to meet your identified needs, get out your calendar and schedule a visit with each group. This process can take time, but that is fine. There is no rush or hurry in this process. It is important that you take whatever time you need to select a support group that will provide you with the safe place you deserve.

I highly recommend that, from this day on, you attend at least one support group a week. Attending more than one group a week is all the more helpful. Once you have selected a support group, it is critical that you attend regularly. Protect this time for yourself. It is your turn! And you deserve it!

Skill 2:
Selecting a Therapist

Each of us has different needs in selecting a counselor. The following are some of the things I need from my therapist.

1. Freedom from role complications

I need a therapist who is free to care for me without worrying about competing needs or roles. Therefore, I need a therapist who is not also a colleague or a friend. It is important for me that my therapist not rely on me for help in any way. I want to feel free to bring myself to each session without worrying about competing loyalties.

2. Confidence in his or her expertise

I need a therapist who has sufficient training, expertise, and personal warmth to generate a sense of trust within me. I rely on my therapist as a guide into unknown territory. It is therefore critical to me that I have confidence that my therapist has gone into this territory before me and understands the pitfalls and dangers.

3. Compatible worldview

Working with a therapist whose outlook on life is supportive and helpful is a requirement for me. I consider myself a deeply spiritual person, and it is important to me that my therapist understand and help me draw strength from my trust in God. As a woman, I need a therapist who understands the unique issues related to my gender. As an addict, I have need of a realistic and solid presentation of reality in my therapy.

4. Confidence that he or she is free of the Messiah Trap

Perhaps the most important thing for me is working with a therapist who is not also caught in the Messiah Trap. It is not uncommon for the people who are drawn into the fields of mental health, ministry, and support services to be addicted to their helping roles. If I am to escape the Messiah Trap, it is imperative that my therapist be able to set proper self-boundaries on caregiving and to cultivate a balanced personal and spiritual life.

I have described some of the things I need from therapy. Decide what you may need from such a relationship.

What I need from a therapy relationship:

Identifying Obstacles to Participating in Therapy

Asking for help is hard for any of us Messiahs. Asking for "professional" help can be especially difficult because of a variety of real and imagined obstacles. In the same way that it was easy for me to come up with reasons why I didn't need a support group, it is quite simple to list a variety of reasons why I don't need therapy.

Carmen's obstacles:

1. Not enough time: I am spending one hour a week on this workbook and another two hours at a support group meeting. How could I possibly find the time for therapy?

2. Not enough money: At least the support group is free! I don't have the money to pay for a therapist. I have responsibilities and I have already pledged a large portion of my income to several charity organizations.

3. I'm not crazy: Only people in serious difficulty go to a therapist. I may have some problems with helping, but I'm not that bad.

My obstacles to participating in therapy:

Overcoming Obstacles to Participating in Therapy

Over the past several years I have traveled all over the United States giving presentations on the topic of escaping the Messiah Trap. After my workshops, many people have come up to talk with me about their recovery journeys. It is interesting to me to see how many of us have trouble taking care of ourselves in loving, balanced ways. Again and again I hear people say, "I know I need to take better care of myself, but . . ." They may fill in the blank with words such as:

- "My job is too demanding."
- "I have small children at home."
- "I have a sick parent who needs me."

Escaping the Messiah Trap

- "I don't have the money I need, so I have to work this hard."
- "I am married and my spouse is very demanding."

There seems to be an endless list of reasons why we can't take care of ourselves.

I believe that if all these reasons could be boiled down to their commonalities, there would be only two—that each person feels overly responsible for the care of others (Lie 1: If I don't do it, it won't get done) and also feels obligated to put his or her needs last (Lie 2: Everyone else's needs take priority over mine).

When I look over my list of obstacles to therapy, it is easy for me to see that they are all rooted in the lies of the Messiah Trap. I do not believe I have enough time for therapy because I feel obligated to allocate my time to the care of others, not to myself. My view of money is very similar to my view of time. I spend my money on the things I value. While I do not have money to burn (and I realize that many of us in the Messiah Trap are working in jobs in which we are horribly *under*paid), I do have choices about how to set my priorities. Once I set a goal, you can be certain I will reach that goal—somehow, someday. I can be very dedicated and competent when I set my mind to something.

Most of the Messiahs I know are also very competent and disciplined people. We will fight for our causes and work diligently for the welfare of others. If I have a friend who has a material need, I am the first to find some extra cash to cover that person's tab. Many of us have learned how to raise large sums of money for worthy causes through our jobs, churches, synagogues, service clubs, and community groups. But when it comes to meeting our own material needs, especially if it means redirecting finances, it is not uncommon for us to sound helpless and hindered by a so-called lack of funds.

The fundamental issue, as I see it, is one of commitment. Once we acknowledge our need and right to therapy, we Messiahs can be extremely resourceful people. There are a variety of ways to locate the necessary funds for therapy. Some of us have insurance that will cover part of the expense. Many therapists in private practice have sliding scales and may offer you an affordable fee. In most communities there are mental health clinics and centers that provide low-cost therapy. One friend was so resourceful that, for his birthday and Christmas, he informed his friends and family that those who wanted could contribute to his therapy fund.

The way we choose to spend our money, perhaps as much as the way we choose to spend our time, illustrates what we value. If we value ourselves and our recovery, our commitment will be illustrated by spending time and finances on ourselves in healthy ways. The converse is also true. Our addiction will leave its mark on an overly crowded schedule and a budget that gives too much away.

My third objection to therapy (that I am not crazy) is similar to one of my objections to attending a support group. If you remember, I didn't want to go to a support group because I didn't want to admit that I was "in that bad a shape." This is yet another form of the Messiah lies—that people who ask for help are inferior and defective.

The fact of the matter is, participating in therapy is not an indicator of "craziness" or inferiority or weakness. To the contrary, pretending we don't need help and denying ourselves what we need is an indicator of weakness. It takes courage and strength to face the truth and take care of ourselves.

I urge you to honestly assess the obstacles to therapy that you listed to see if they are valid or if they are yet another expression of the Messiah lies.

Assessment of my obstacles to therapy:

Interviewing Therapists

The process I recommend in selecting a therapist is similar to the process of selecting a support group.

Collecting a List of Therapists

Many of us wait until we are desperate, depressed, or burned out before we look for a therapist. Then, out of our intense despair, we grab the first counselor we find. Therapy is like any other intimate relationship. Selection of a therapist, like the selection of a spouse or close friend, warrants time and attention.

The first step is developing a list a therapists. I recommend that you interview several therapists before making a selection. This is to protect you from feeling obligated to stay with the first one you see. I know of people who stay with their therapist, not because they are benefiting from the relationship, but because they don't want to hurt their therapist's feelings by leaving. To avoid this trap, it is critical to collect several names from which to choose.

While I suggested that you use the yellow pages to select a support group, I do not recommend such a procedure for selecting a therapist. Unless you are new to an area and know absolutely no one, it is better to ask around among your friends, colleagues, and acquaintances for names of effective counselors. Although what was helpful to your sister-in-law may not be your cup of tea, such a referral may be a good place to start. Your sister-in-law's therapist may work in a group of therapists, one of whom may be a great match for you.

My list of therapists:

Name: Phone:

_____

_____

_____

_____

_____

Preparing to Interview Therapists

After you have collected your list of possible therapists, the next step is to make some initial phone calls asking for an opportunity to interview them. Be clear with each therapist that you are meeting with several professionals.

If a therapist is offended by this information, feel free to cross that person off your list. A therapist who believes that he or she is competent to treat any and all people may, in fact, be caught in the Messiah Trap. This person may be overly confident about his or her capabilities. In contrast, a more competent therapist will recognize that certain people work better together than others. An initial interview will give both you and the therapist a chance to see if it feels like "a fit."

After you have made appointments with all the therapists on your list, prepare for your interviews by reviewing your list of needs. If you have thought of other needs, add those to your list.

Some additional questions I might add are:

1. Are you being supervised? By whom?

In the mental health system, it is common for a therapist to meet with a supervisor or a group of therapists to talk over cases and receive guidance. I personally would not see a therapist who was not in supervision. For me, this is a possible indication that the therapist is caught in the Messiah Trap.

"Messiah" therapists are those who consider themselves superior to all other therapists and, therefore, no longer in need of learning or guidance. Therapists who are in supervision, by contrast, are more likely to be open to new ideas, up-to-date on current literature and treatment issues, and better able to assess their own mistakes so that they don't damage your progress.

2. Have you had special training in treating addictions or codependency?

The world of psychology is made up of a wide variety of theories and models. Some perspectives reject the notion of addictions as presented in this workbook. It would undermine your progress if you worked with a therapist who was hostile to or belittling of your recovery process.

Other therapists are open to issues of addiction but have received little or no training in treating such clients. I wouldn't advise submitting yourself as a guinea pig for their first learning experience. It could be unnecessarily painful as they make their initial mistakes with you. Instead, find a therapist with solid experience and training in treating codependency and addictions.

3. What are your credentials? Please describe to me your philosophy of treatment.

This is a very important question because you can learn a great deal from both the content of the answer and the way the answer is given. A therapist who is insecure or inattentive may give you an answer full of jargon and vocabulary that is confusing or intimidating. If you cannot understand the answer, it is important to remember that the fault does not lie with you. To the contrary, it is the therapist's job to know how to meet you at your point of need and communicate effectively with you. One who confuses you in an initial interview is not a therapist you can count on in the long run.

If the therapist clearly explains his or her approach to therapy so that you feel respected, you have probably found someone who will treat you with the dignity you deserve throughout the therapy process. If the therapist has a perspective that contradicts your own, that must be noted as a misfit. Most likely, however, a therapist who honors your dignity and can clearly explain what he or she can offer you is someone capable of traveling with you through the recovery journey.

Preparing a Summary Statement for Participating in Therapy

Last, before you attend your first session, prepare to tell the therapist what you want to accomplish in therapy. It may be helpful to write out your thoughts beforehand so that you will feel confident of your goals.

My reason for participating in therapy:

Interviewing therapists and making my selection:

In the following space, write out your assessment of each interview. Once you have interviewed all the therapists on your list, select the best match and commit yourself to regular sessions.

*The Twelve Steps of Alcoholics Anonymous**

1. We admitted we were powerless over alcohol—that our lives had become unmanageable.

2. Came to believe that a Power greater than ourselves could restore us to sanity.

3. Made a decision to turn our will and our lives over to the care of God *as we understood Him.*

4. Made a searching and fearless moral inventory of ourselves.

5. Admitted to God, to ourselves, and to another human being the exact nature of our wrongs.

6. Were entirely ready to have God remove all these defects of character.

7. Humbly asked Him to remove our shortcomings.

8. Made a list of all persons we had harmed, and became willing to make amends to them all.

9. Made direct amends to such people wherever possible, except when to do so would injure them or others.

10. Continued to take personal inventory and when we were wrong promptly admitted it.

11. Sought through prayer and meditation to improve our conscious contact with God *as we understood Him,* praying only for knowledge of His will for us and the power to carry that out.

12. Having had a spiritual awakening as the result of these steps, we tried to carry this message to alcoholics, and to practice these principles in all our affairs.

---

*Twelve Steps from the book *Alcoholics Anonymous,* © 1939, 1955, 1976, Alcoholics Anonymous World Services, Inc. Reprinted by permission.